Praise for J

NEVER EVEI

MW01717524

"An inspirational story about a first-generation immigrant rising to become a Fortune 500 CEO, raising emotionally healthy and successful children, and sharing his philosophy of humility, gratitude, authenticity, and happiness. A must-read for all, including all parents."

—Tal Ben-Shahr, Author and Teacher, New York Times bestselling author

"This book brings the American dream to life! A fascinating story about leadership, authenticity, commitment to values, and beliefs about free enterprise and what America offers to those who have a vision — and never ever give up."

—Pete Hegseth, Anchor of Friends and Family on Fox and New York Times bestselling author

"A magnificent American Dream story, and every word is true. Inspiring and life changing."

—John Arnold, Former Founder and CEO of Petroleum Products Corp., Philanthropist

"With little more than a backpack and a dream, Jay Sidhu started off on a journey that took him from his native India through Afghanistan, Iran, Europe, and eventually to the United States, where he rose to the top of the banking industry. What a fascinating life, and what a fascinating book."

—Steve Zuckerman, Principal and CEO, Oaktree Development Corp.

"A leadership book like no other. Jay Sidhu brings out the best in his coworkers, team members, and investors. In this book, he'll bring out the best in you."

—Mike Pavone, President Founder & CEO Pavone Marketing Group

"Jay Sidhu is that rare leader who creates not only followers but other leaders. You will learn from and love this book."

—Jay Cleveland, President and CEO, Cleveland Brothers

Praise for Jay Sidhu's book

NEVER EVER, *EVER* GIVE UP

"No money? No connections? You could still go to the top. Let Jay Sidhu show you how." —*Dave Bhasin, Founder and CEO, Multiconcept Group, Inc.*

"Jay Sidhu arrived in the United States with little more than two suitcases and a desire to better himself. Not only did he create his own life journey, but he provided employment to thousands and his innovations transformed the banking industry. I loved reading his story."

—*Mike Robinson, Owner and President, Founder PAP Technologies, Inc.*

"Jay Sidhu, his son, and his daughter have all been CEOs of New York Stock Exchange-traded companies. Find out what drives their success in this outstanding leadership book."

—*Max Hempt, Entrepreneur & Former President & CEO, Hempt Brothers*

"Jay Sidhu proves that nice guys finish first. If you think business success requires a dog-eat-dog attitude, Jay will show you that there is a better way."

—*John Ortenzio, President CEO, Select Capital Corp.*

"Jay Sidhu grew up in India, received his higher education in the United States, and built a great career for himself with the broadest possible definition of success—work, finance, family, service. Jay is a role model."

—*Boris Levin, CEO, Stargate Capital Corp., Munich, Germany*

"The title *Never Ever, Ever Give Up*, symbolizes Jay's can-do attitude. Hard work, persistence, a heady brew of positive thinking getting extremely positive results. A must-read leadership book."

—*Marc Grossman, CEO, Founder & Chairman, Celio Group Paris*

"An excellent leadership book, full of inspiration and wisdom from a lifetime of experience. A must-read for all aspiring students, entrepreneurs, managers, parents and leaders. This will be a must-read for all at Sidhu School."

—*Dean Adekola of Sidhu School of Business and Leadership*

NEVER EVER, *EVER* GIVE UP

NEVER EVER, *EVER* GIVE UP

An inspiring true story about leadership, commitment, resiliency, happiness and making your dreams come true

JAY SIDHU

WAHEGURU PRESS
Los Angeles, California

Hardcover: ISBN 979-8-9873367-0-0

Paperback: ISBN 979-8-9873367-1-7

Ebook: 979-8-9873367-2-4

Audiobook: ISBN 979-8-9873367-3-1

First Edition, 2022

Publisher's Cataloging-In-Publication

Names: Sidhu, Jay, author.

Title: Never ever , ever give up : an inspiring true story about leadership, commitment, resiliency, happiness and making your dreams come true / Jay Sidhu.

Description: Includes bibliographical references. | Los Angeles, CA: Waheguru Press, 2023.

Identifiers: LCCN: 2022922041 | ISBN: 979-8-9873367-0-0 (hardcover) | 979-8-9873367-1-7 (paper-back) | 979-8-9873367-2-4 (ebook) | 979-8-9873367-3-1 (audio)

Subjects: LCSH Sidhu, Jay. | Bankers--Biography. | Self-actualization (Psychology) | Leadership. | BISAC BIOGRAPHY & AUTOBIOGRAPHY / Personal Memoirs | BIOGRAPHY & AUTOBIOGRAPHY / Business | BUSINESS & ECONOMICS / Leadership | BUSINESS & ECONOMICS / Banks & Banking

Classification: LCC HG2463 .S53 2023 | DDC 332.1/23/092--dc23

Printed in the United States of America on acid-free paper.

Cover author photo: Tony Mercado

Cover and book design: Patricia Bacall, bacallcreative.com

Interior photos courtesy of the author.

WAHEGURU PRESS

Los Angeles, California

All the proceeds from the sale of this book are being donated to

SidhuFamilyCharity.org

This book is dedicated to my parents, my wife Sherry, our children Samvir and Luvleen and their spouses Linda and Brian, my colleagues and friends and Forum Brothers.

Really appreciate your support and encouragement throughout my life.

CONTENTS

Foreword

It has been my great pleasure to have known Jay since 1986. We first met when Jay was hired to turn around the troubled Penn Savings Bank where I was a member of the board of directors. Jay's unique blend of financial expertise, marketing savvy, and leadership qualities made him the ideal candidate for the job. Our collegial relationship has continued to this day, as I now serve the Lead Independent Director for Customers Bancorp, where Jay is the Chairman and CEO.

I'm delighted he has shared his personal story, business experiences, and lifetime learnings in this book. He's gone from being the son of a Sikh Indian military officer to a young man emigrating to America, earning an MBA, and first leading Sovereign Bancorp from a $400 million troubled bank with a market cap of only $12 million to the 17th largest bank in the US with assets of about $90 billion and a market cap of $12 billion at the time of his retirement. During his tenure at Sovereign, he achieved greater than 20 percent average annual returns for the shareholders.

Today, in round two, he took over a failing $200 million asset bank with no equity left and transformed Customers Bancorp into a $20 billion asset bank at the forefront of digital banking, again achieving greater than 20 percent average annual returns for the shareholders.

This book is about much more than a typical immigrant's success story. It's a compelling narrative with instructive lessons on strategic vision and execution. It demonstrates how to lead with positivity, humility, diplomacy, and smarts. But perhaps most importantly, it shows the value of perseverance and integrity.

Dan Rothermel
Former General Council of Carpenter Technology
CEO of Cumru Associates
Lead Independent Director for Sovereign Bancorp & Customers Bancorp

Foreword

Jay and I have a long, colorful history together, dating back to June of 1973. I clearly remember the date because the dean of students at Wilkes University called to let me know he had an exceptional MBA graduate looking to get into the financial services industry. I was working at First Valley Bank at the time, but the hiring cycle for its management training program was December, and this was June. Nevertheless, I told the dean we would happily meet with Jay. Reese Jones, our president, and I knew right away there was something tremendously special about Jay. So we convinced him to join us in helping build First Valley Bank's business.

Jay is a talented banker with enormous potential. And at various points in his career, he felt stuck and ready for new challenges. The happy result was that Jay and I worked together at First Valley, Sovereign Bancorp and most recently, Customers Bancorp. As he assumed new roles and his career trajectory continued upward, we stayed in touch and found ways to work together.

Jay is a brilliant strategist, a true visionary leader. He has a gift for allowing others the freedom to chart their own course while, at the same time providing safety guardrails to ensure he'll achieve his endgame. I also witnessed Jay navigate some sticky boardroom politics with finesse and success.

It's a privilege for me to count Jay among my very closest friends. He's an authentic individual and an exceptional human being. Some people say that with each position Jay held, he changed. I say the man never changed. He just became a lot wiser.

Richard Ehst
Former President & CEO of Customers Bank

Introduction

THE PARTITION OF INDIA... AND MY PARENTS CAUGHT IN THE MIDDLE

AUGUST 1951.

I was born shortly after one of the most horrendous periods in the recent history of the Indian subcontinent. This book is about my life story, some lessons learned along the way, and my conviction never ever to give up on achieving your vision and mission.

AUGUST 1947.

Blood and bodies strewn everywhere. A night train hurtling from West Pakistan to India. Suddenly, the train stops. Pakistani soldiers and civilians come on board. In a matter of minutes, all the men are slaughtered. All the women and girls are kidnapped and raped.

My newlywed parents were on board the train immediately following and witnessed what happened. Mercifully, they showed no physical scars, just hidden emotional ones. And my father, Lieutenant Bhag Singh Sidhu, demonstrated the level-headed preparation and resolve that characterized his entire life.

My father had been commissioned into what was then called the British Indian Army near the end of World War II. He served in Burma and was on patrol in a forest when he was wounded by a Japanese soldier's grenade.

After the war, Dad was assigned to a storied regiment of the British Indian Army infantry called the Frontier Force Rifles, which patrolled the Afghan border near the northeastern city of Abbottabad. (Abbottabad, of course, is now well known as the town where Osama bin Laden was killed in 2011.) Dad served alongside all types of Indians—Hindus, Muslims, Christians, and Sikhs like himself.

My dad met my mother, Dhanwant Grewal, through an arranged marriage—a very common occurrence among Indian families at that time. A mutual friend would say something like, "There's a family nearby, and that family has a kid close to the same age as yours. Let's introduce them?" When arranged marriages take place in India today, it's more like an introduction, sort of like a blind date. But back then, the parents would look at the other family's background, ask about their values and such, and then the young people would meet and, most likely, marry.

My parents were married in February 1947. My dad was twenty-three, a second lieutenant in the army. My mom was seventeen, a smart, religious young woman from a family of doctors. I have a picture from when they got married, with him in his uniform, the two stars on his shoulder denoting the rank of second lieutenant.

After they married, my mom went to live with my dad in a tribal area of Abbottabad, where Dad was stationed. Like every officer, Dad was given a house. When he'd go out on active duty, my mom would stay in Abbottabad. As a young married woman, she would have a solider stationed nearby as a guard.

On August 14, 1947, just a few months after they were married, my Dad rushed home. When he got there, he said to my mom, "We've got to get out of here!"

After some three hundred years in India and eighty-nine years of official colonial rule, the British Empire (or British Raj, as the UK's government in India was called) was finally giving India back its independence. India was being partitioned, and the Islamic Republic of Pakistan was created for the Muslim minority.

That led to a massive political and religious split. People were separated on the basis of religion, a division that had been growing for decades in India under the British and really boiled over during World War II.

The Partition of India saw some of the most horrific violence of the twentieth century—there were mass rapes, abductions, dismemberment, and murder on both sides on a genocidal scale. Villages were set on fire.

Millions of people—including pregnant women and children—were killed.

There was no law and order. Most people who lived through that deadly, terrible time in India don't want to think about it today. I've spoken to many different people—my friends' parents, and my mom and dad's contemporaries—who lived in India and Pakistan then. They may talk a little bit about that time, but then they want to move on. They don't want to dwell on it.

The Partition of India brought about one of the largest mass migrations in human history. Over six million Muslims went from India to Pakistan, and millions of Hindus and Sikhs moved from West Pakistan to India. About 12 million people were displaced amid the ensuing violence. Pakistan's leaders essentially said, "Get rid of anybody in Pakistan who is non-Muslim. If they don't want to go, convert them. And if they don't want to convert ... kill them." On the other hand, India became a secular country. (In 1976, the 42nd Amendment to the Indian Constitution explicitly asserted India's secularism.)

As the horror began, word came from Dad's headquarters that trouble was on the way and that it was the responsibility of his battalion to make sure that all non-Muslims, including Sikhs like him and my mom, were protected. The officers in Dad's unit basically told the non-Muslims that the situation was unfortunate, but they had to get out immediately.

Mom and Dad, who were on the other side of the area of what was now Pakistan, left on a train immediately to get to the Indian border, part of the mass migration out of the Muslim territory. At the time, my mom was a naïve seventeen-year-old girl who had never been out of India.

Mom described to me how she saw blood and bodies everywhere. She says she could never, ever forget that. But she says that on the train, my dad said to her, "Don't worry about anything. Go to sleep, get some rest. My army colleagues and I are here to protect every family, everybody here. We will do anything and everything to make sure we get safely across the border into India."

My parents were on the train all night. Everywhere in Pakistan, Pakistani soldiers and civilians were stopping transports filled with non-Muslims; they were boarding the trains and killing people. Because of the danger, every time my parents' train slowed down during the night, my dad and the other soldiers around him would jump up with their guns.

Then suddenly, in the early morning hours … the train stopped.

My dad and his fellow soldiers used signal communications with walkie-talkies to talk to the other officers in the other sections, so they knew something was happening on both ends of the train. There were violent massacres in the train cars in front of and behind the car my parents were on. The Pakistanis went from car to car, and if the train didn't move soon, the people in the middle section—including my mom and dad—would likely be killed.

The entire train was surrounded by attackers, but the compartment my mom and dad were on, the middle one, just happened to have nearly a full Indian army company on it. They were the fortunate ones —the others on this transport didn't have that kind of protection, or the Indian army soldiers on those cars were outnumbered, and so the Pakistanis slaughtered them. They killed all the men and dragged the young women and girls off those train cars. They raped them and then took them away to convert them to Islam.

Almost all the people on those trains were either kidnapped or killed.

While the attack was going on, the Pakistanis became aware of the radio contact among the officers on the train. They had been informed that an Indian military unit was coming, so they knew it would be all military people and their families on this transport.

Word quickly got out to the marauders that there was one train car in the middle with almost a full army unit on board. Perhaps that's why my parents' train car was never attacked. Had it been boarded, the Indian army soldiers on the train would probably have killed as many Pakistanis as they could before they died themselves. That possibility bought them time, and soon the engineers got the train moving again. The marauders never got to the middle section, and my parents were able to continue on to India—and safety.

My parents' life-or-death experience, just a few months into their marriage, affected them deeply, and that effect was passed on to me. On that train, my dad's personal mission was to get to safety at all costs, to focus on surviving, and to do anything necessary to achieve his goals. Dad knew when he boarded that train from Abbottabad to India that he would need to have a clear vision if he and my mother were going to survive. Most importantly, he had the conviction to never ever give up on achieving that mission. I've embraced my father's lessons with the result that I've done more than survive. I've thrived.

When the train got to India, my dad's battalion was assigned the responsibility of helping all the people who were arriving at the Indian border point, getting them over to refugee camps, aiding people who were lost, and assisting anyone looking for missing relatives. Dad assigned one of his soldiers who was leaving the border site to escort my mom to Barnala, in the state of Punjab, which is the heart of India's Sikh community. My mom's father, a physician, was stationed as the chief medical officer in Barnala at that time.

My brother was born later in 1949, and I was born two years after him in 1951. As an officer in the Indian army during the Indian-Pakistani conflict, my father was always on alert, ready to fight at any moment or to maintain peace, as necessary. There was no way to reach him when my mom went into labor with me.

During that time, my mom lived with my grandma and aunt. The only way to get to the hospital was to take a tonga, which is similar to a rickshaw but driven by a horse, with a canopied carriage that fits four people. So that's how the three women traveled.

I couldn't wait to be born and arrived on the tonga wrapped in my grandmother's lightweight shawl. We never even got to the hospital and instead turned around and went back home. One of my parent's neighbors was a midwife, and they left the rest to her.

I grew up primarily at military cantonments across India and also lived with my uncle, an eye doctor in Patiala, Punjab. I went to nine different schools before graduating from Cambridge University through Yadavindra Public Schools (YPS) in Patiala. Fortunately, I was always able to adjust easily to new places and new people. And I had a vision of traveling throughout the world and studying in the United States.

My dreams were very much influenced by my cousin Sher Sidhu, who found a way from a village in Punjab to graduate from the University of Michigan and become a successful entrepreneur. My brother also followed in his footsteps and, after several twists and turns, also studied at the University of Michigan. However, I found myself being pressured by my mom, dad, uncles, and aunts to either become a doctor or join the Army and settle in India.

However, I never ever gave up on my vision, despite many setbacks and failures. Dad would have been proud of that. Sadly, he didn't live long enough to see it.

Chapter 1

A LIFE-CHANGING JOURNEY

What could be more exciting and pleasurable than traveling across Europe and Asia with your college friend when you're just eighteen years old? When we think about visiting cities like Teheran, Istanbul, Athens, or London, we imagine ourselves staying in youth hostels or inexpensive hotels, meeting lots of other people our age, going out for great meals, and relying on train passes to get from one city to the next.

Now imagine the same trip, but this time without money, without youth hostels, without hearty meals, and without train passes. Instead, you're hitchhiking mainly with truckers, sometimes for days at a stretch. You're barely eating because you've got exactly $100 in your pocket, and it has to last for the entire trip, from Kabul, Afghanistan, all the way to London and back to India. You're sleeping on the ground or on the sidewalk, not on beds with fresh linen, to save money, curled over your backpack to ensure that your clothing and worldly goods aren't stolen. Train passes? Forget about it!

This is how Gautam, a classmate and friend at Banaras Hindu University, and I crossed from India to London when I was just eighteen years old. We were naïve about the dangers, but somehow, we were protected, even when our lives were threatened on a dusty road in Afghanistan, and we found ourselves in jail in Paris. Somehow, it all worked out, and we had the adventure of a lifetime. That trip gave me the courage to pursue my dreams in life, come to America and study, and make something of myself. I'd like to invite you on that journey fifty years ago when my friend and I set out on a mission to spread the idea of international peace and understanding.

A rare meal of bread with butter was a huge treat. I was terrified much of the time, and often, I was lost. But on occasion, I met kind people who generously helped me; many were simply trying to survive, but they still shared with open hearts.

If I had known the difficulties and dangers ahead, it's doubtful I would have left India and hitchhiked across continents. But I am so very, very glad I did. I discovered the excitement of taking risks and achieving extraordinary outcomes. I gained the confidence and sense of invincibility to confront challenges and overcome them. I became motivated to literally expand my horizons and travel abroad. And I learned that I was adaptable and resourceful.

My experiences also taught me that my father, whom you'll meet in these pages, was right that by defining a mission and setting forth a step-by-step strategy to achieve it and even exceed expectations, I could succeed in life. I'm sharing these memories so that they might inspire you to take some chances and succeed in ways *you* might never have imagined!

I went from being the son of an infantry officer in the Indian army and a stay-at-home mom to earning an MBA in America and, eventually, becoming the Chief Executive Officer of a failing bank that I led to become a Fortune 500 powerhouse in the US financial services industry.

This is more than a story of a backpacking expedition of two young, naïve boys. It's also a story of how America is, indeed, a "land of opportunity" that offers everyone worldwide, regardless of origin, a chance to follow their dreams and make those dreams come true.

❁❁❁

My father trusted me to drive a military Jeep when I was ten years old. As a high-ranking infantry officer in the Indian army, he would drive a Jeep home from the office. I thought the vehicle was very cool and asked to drive it. He agreed, so I hopped into the passenger seat, and he drove about 100 yards. I watched him maneuver the stick shift, paying particular attention to the movements of his hands and feet. Then, he asked if I was ready to drive, and I answered with a resounding "yes."

I almost landed in a ditch, but thankfully, I was able to apply the brakes. My father didn't criticize me. He didn't berate me. Instead, he said, "OK, son, so you've learned a lesson." And on his subsequent visits home, he'd let me drive for three minutes, then four, then five.

My father taught me that life is all about planning your mission and achieving it successfully. And to never ever give up along the way, even if you face adversity. He stressed the critical importance of defining your mission clearly and succinctly. "What are you trying to achieve?" (Drive safely.) Next, determine the steps necessary to achieve that objective. "How will you win your mission?" (Trust, observe, and practice.) Along the way, evaluate the steps and listen to feedback. "Is it advisable to pivot strategically?" (Take a different vehicle or a different route.) And no matter what, never take your mind off your vision or your dream.

Through his example, my father showed me how resilience is a key attribute of being both a successful human being and an effective leader. Learn from your failures and celebrate your successes. Motivate yourself and your team with enthusiasm and passion. That's how everyone, yourself included, will enjoy achieving your mission. And I sure enjoyed my subsequent driving adventures.

By the time I was twelve years old, I had perfected my driving skills, and it's fortuitous that I did. There was an emergency that required my mother and grandmother to travel about five hours away from our house in Delhi. My father wasn't home, and my mother couldn't drive. My dad's driving lessons served me well, and there I was in the driver's seat of our Fiat car, making the long trek without falling into a ditch.

I was making great progress on my mission, and there was more to come. When I was fourteen, my uncle, my mom's sister's husband, wanted to take his Vespa scooter to Delhi on the same route, and I volunteered to drive alone. At first, my uncle refused, but he relented with a compromise: he would accompany me on the back seat. The scooter's top speed was about 45 kilometers per hour, but I fearlessly drove from Patiala to Delhi at the risky rate of about 60 kilometers per hour. I drove so fast that my uncle's turban blew off! It was wintertime, and I still remember my hands vibrating on the scooter's handles and the frigid air whipping at my mask-less face. My body was numb from the cold by the time we arrived, but I felt exhilarated. What an awesome eight-hour experience for a fourteen-year-old boy!

Thanks to my father, my thrilling adventures continued in high school. One winter, my father was commanding his infantry regiment in Leh, near the Chinese and Pakistan border. My dad always wrote short letters home while he was away, and one described how cold it was and how his convoy of infantrymen had to drive along unpaved roads with walls of six to twelve feet of icy snow on either side, like a frozen wind tunnel.

The prospect of another driving escapade with my father was irresistible, and I asked to visit him in Leh. My dad hesitated because you weren't allowed to take civilians on the route, but again, he agreed to take me. We went in his military Jonga, the Indian equivalent of a Humvee, and had a blast together, sliding and skidding on the icy road.

Not only did my dad nurture my spirit of adventure, but he also gave me confidence by treating me as an adult. He was the most significant influence on my life, teaching me lessons about kindness, leadership, discipline, and more. He constantly modeled and reinforced his message that to be a great leader, you must first be a great human being.

I admire how he made his way up from humble beginnings. He was one of six children and the only one who went to college. His siblings remained in the farming business. My dad attended St. Joseph's College, a military academy in India, on his own initiative. Since World War II was still raging, the Indian military offered accelerated commissions, and he quickly rose to become an officer in the infantry division.

My father was so highly respected by his unit, the Dogras Infantry Regiment, that his peers nominated him to be the commandant. He returned that respect in his dealings with his unit. In the Indian Army, like the British Army, officers were assigned orderlies. These soldiers stayed with you, took care of you, and helped you in any way necessary. But my dad never treated his orderlies like servants or inferior soldiers; he treated them like family, with appreciation and generosity.

Although he was a man of few words, my father was extremely personable. When he said something, it was worth listening to. He set firm limits for me and communicated them clearly. For two short years, I attended Delhi

Public School, a prestigious private high school in Delhi. Once, my father was called by the headmaster to pick me up for a behavioral infraction. The school was very strict. There was a system whereby you would get a yellow card for an academic violation and a red card for a behavioral problem. If you received three yellow or three red cards, you were kicked out of school.

The incident involved a few of my friends in a chemistry class and me. We thought it would be funny to take some foul-smelling gases and put them in the vents of our headmaster's air conditioner. The whole place stank, and we got caught. As punishment, my father was called to the school to pick me up. He came, this imposing man in a military uniform, and looked me in the eye, saying, "make sure I am *never, ever* asked to come to your school again." That was it. No yelling, no beating, no being grounded. Just a clear, straightforward statement that expressed his expectations.

My parents balanced each other. Although both were disciplined, my father took calculated risks, whereas my mother valued academic rigor. My father always treated me like an adult, whereas my mother protected me like a child. As I stated in the introduction, they had an arranged marriage in 1947 when my father was in his early 20s, and my mother was only 17. That was when the British left, and the subcontinent was partitioned into two states: Hindu-majority India and Muslim-majority Pakistan. (My family adheres to Sikhism.)

The region became a bloodbath during partition some 75 years ago, and my parents witnessed the horrific violence and killing. Every day, they didn't know if they would survive another one. What a way to begin their young married life! They rarely talked about the atrocities they saw, but their experiences brought them closer together. Even as a child, I knew they loved each other.

My parents had a conventional relationship in that my dad worked, and my mom managed the household. She was naïve and depended on him with absolute trust that he would take care of her. Their backgrounds were very different. While my father's family was lower-middle class and not college-educated, my mother's father and brothers were all physicians. My mother also wanted to attend medical school, but like most in her culture, her parents decided to marry her off instead.

A traditional Indian woman, my mother was exceedingly intelligent and principled. She was very strict with herself and with me. Every morning, to this day, at 92 years old, she gets up at 5:00 a.m., takes a cold shower, and prays. She expected similarly disciplined behavior from me. When she woke me up one morning, insisting that I study for an algebra test, I was not a happy camper. At 6:00 a.m., she came into my room again, and she wasn't happy either. I told her I was studying, and she firmly said, "how can you be studying? I don't see a notebook, and I don't see a pen. Next time you study, you will have a notebook, pens, an eraser, and a timer." Neither of my parents minced words.

Although my mother constantly pushed me, my academic career wasn't stellar. My father's role in the military required us to move frequently, so the maximum time we spent in one place was the three-and-a-half years that he was stationed at the Indian army headquarters in Delhi. Prior to university, I attended nine different schools.

When I'm asked how I seamlessly adjusted so often to different environments, schools, and friends, I answer honestly that I didn't know there was any other way of life. Instead of feeling that moving represented challenging upheavals, I viewed them as exciting opportunities. Perhaps my personality is inherently extroverted, but I wasn't intimidated by exploring new places and meeting new people. I wasn't afraid to make the first move to introduce myself and engage in conversation. Like so many of my childhood experiences, adjusting to new social situations prepared me well for my career.

Developing and maintaining positive interpersonal relationships continues to be a crucial element in my success. Of course, it's not enough to be able to reach out and smile and make small talk to succeed in business; it requires nurturing respect for others' perspectives, cultivating empathy, and listening to the subtext. And it also requires education, at home, on the job, or in the classroom.

My mother wanted me to follow the path of the men in her family and pursue a medical degree. She encouraged me to talk to my uncles, who were physicians, and they almost persuaded me to go to medical school. My dad encouraged me to consider an army career, but I didn't want to get stuck in the military. There were three standard career choices for Indian Sikhs with my background: the military, medicine, or engineering. No one in my family was in business. But my ambition since childhood was to go to the United States to study business. Later, that dream was fulfilled.

In the interim, there was a one-year program after high school with a pre-med track, and I decided to give it a try. What a disaster! I simply couldn't memorize facts and (what I considered irrelevant) details. Understanding, yes. Analyzing, yes. Memorizing, no.

My father demonstrated the importance of authenticity, along with the need for structure. I continually re-evaluated my goals, objectives, and performance and pivoted whenever necessary. It was time to pivot away from the goal of becoming a physician. My new mission was to become a businessman.

My father gave me a valuable personal and professional education, but I also wanted a formal business education. It wasn't difficult for my cousin, who lived in the United States, to convince me that the US had the best business educational system in the world. I eventually ended up in the graduate business management program at Wilkes University in Wilkes-Barre, Pennsylvania, and earned an MBA there. But first, I needed to apply, and my strategy was to prepare a compelling application to gain admission.

Like my father, I take risks. Like both my parents, I don't mince words. The gist of my Wilkes University application essay discussed how business leaders could change India. In retrospect, that may seem like a naïve position, but I laid out a coherent argument: bureaucracy and poor management lead to inefficiencies, while a leadership education is the path to problem-solving and forward progress. I was taking a risk by criticizing how business and government were conducted in India, but I've always been straightforward; it's a matter of authenticity.

The Wilkes University graduate program complemented my father's invaluable lessons about leadership, which form the core principles of my personal and professional interactions. For example, he demonstrated the qualities that make a successful leader, comprising listening, empathizing, dealing with people respectfully and fairly, and persisting. I applied the structure my father used as a military officer to all aspects of my life, including my self-improvement, interpersonal relationships, and business approach. And I say with great humility that these methods yielded success.

My overarching principle is that personal development is just as important as professional excellence. Understand that you can't do 25 things well, but you can definitely excel at three to four things. Focus on those, and don't give up until you excel at them. Define your personal mission just like you define your professional one.

Managers who focus primarily on numbers and charts often miss the point; winners primarily concentrate on the excitement of the ride and interpersonal relationships. Successful leaders, organizations, teams, individuals, and even successful families all depend on personal self-awareness and group assessments. Further, you don't have to love all the people you work with, but you need to respect and trust them. Just like my father treated his orderly with sensitivity, so, too, should you treat those you work with, your superiors and your supervisees alike. Then, there's no limit to what you'll achieve.

My business success resulted from adhering to these principles. At 37, I became chief operating officer at Sovereign Bancorp, Inc. and Sovereign Bank, a company that didn't have substantial capital resources, nor did it have a significant market share. It operated in the tiny city of Wyomissing, Pennsylvania, and I humbly took the company from nothing to a Fortune 500 company. Not bad for a military brat from Delhi who was born on a tonga carriage.

I had the good fortune of coming to America and studying here. Later, I had the privilege, means, and opportunity to give back to Wilkes University, the school that provided me with the tools to succeed in business. I established the Sidhu School of Business and Leadership. The school's overall **mission** is to prepare graduates with "the knowledge, skills, experiences, and passion for leading diverse organizations in the face of dynamic challenges and a rapidly changing global environment." And the school's step-by-step **strategy** is to empower the "development of personal, professional, and leadership skills through scholarship, experiential learning, and community engagement." Consequently, each student at Wilkes is required to create and implement a personal and professional development plan. Unlike many other BBA and MBA programs, the curriculum stresses leadership. It consists of much more than passing an economics or accounting class; it requires experiential learning and giving back to the community, principally through volunteer work. This well-rounded approach forms leaders. And leaders are change-makers, decision-makers, and oftentimes, money-makers.

It has been a long journey, geographically, personally, professionally, and educationally. But I've derived satisfaction every step of the way. I'm committed to continuing to make great strides and progress in my lifelong adventure. And I will never ever give up on this vision.

Chapter 2

MEETING INDIRA GANDHI... AND SURVIVING AFGHANISTAN

Our hitchhiking trip began in the most unusual of places for a couple of teenagers to find themselves: the office of the prime minister of India, the legendary Indira Gandhi. How do two 18-year-olds find their way to the most powerful person in the land? And then have the chutzpah to ask her to have the Indian government help fund our trip? Let me explain.

When my friend Gautam and I were ushered into an enormous office, a black and white-haired woman wearing a white sari with a red border stood up to greet us. This was unusual because people don't show respect this way in India, especially not to a couple of kids. Her behavior was even more surprising because the woman was neither a secretary nor a government aide; she was the prime minister of India, Indira Gandhi herself.

I later realized that she hadn't risen to greet *us*. Rather, she had risen for Pandit Shiv Prashad, a respected member of parliament in the Congress Party, whose influence had secured us the meeting. He was the father of a great friend of mine at school who we had enlisted to use his position to get us an audience with Indira Gandhi. Why? We purported to solicit government support for our mission to raise awareness among youth and combat the prejudicial views held worldwide that Indians were a bunch of strange, primitive fanatics. We wanted to show that we were the same as civilized, educated, normal American and European kids. The truth was we had no grand schemes for world peace; we were just 18-year-old kids who wanted travel money to hitchhike to London.

As I entered her chambers in new clothes bought specially for the occasion, I was sweating profusely with nervousness. After all, Indira Gandhi was considered a goddess in India.

Before we entered her enormous office, the gatekeeper assistant asked why we were there. I mustered my courage, swallowed, and repeated the line I'd rehearsed many times in my head, "We want to promote peace through international understanding, and we're here with my friend's father to get help." This boldness added to my newly developing self-confidence.

In the prime minister's office, Pandit Prashad introduced us to her in Hindi, explaining that Gautam and I were classmates at Banaras Hindu University and were doing something really intriguing that could potentially help with international relations. He continued, explaining that we needed money to travel and would also appreciate introductions to ambassadors at embassies throughout Asia and Europe along the way.

Prime Minister Gandhi greeted us warmly and surprised us with hugs. I couldn't believe how down-to-earth and straightforward she was. She told us she doubted we could get money since we weren't government officials, but she could certainly introduce us to Indian embassy representatives. She instructed her assistant to write letters on our behalf. But I wanted more.

I cleared my throat again and spoke up. I said, "Thank you very much, Prime Minister, but we will be carrying the flags of India and the United Nations and don't want to be beggars. We should go to the embassies and represent our country with dignity. We could buy the dollars." (At that time, Indians traveling abroad could only convert $8.00 because India's system was deficient in foreign money exchange.) Again, Prime Minister Gandhi instructed her assistant to see what he could do. This was a huge leap toward executing our plan.

She didn't ask me any follow-up questions, but even better, she agreed to let us take pictures with her using my clunky black camera. I was ecstatic about this once-in-a-lifetime opportunity. (Sadly, I lost that picture and all the other photos from our trip in the horrendous flooding of Wilkes Barre during Hurricane Agnes in 1972.)

What a fantastic conclusion to our meeting. It lasted less than five minutes, but every millisecond was thrilling.

My friend's father's influence extended beyond getting us the meeting in New Delhi. As a member of parliament, he received special consideration and obtained a letter for us to take to a government-authorized bank in Patiala. There was a lot of bureaucracy to navigate, and we were required to put up security. We left India with only $100 (and a few hundred Indian rupees, which had little to no value in Europe in those days). We eventually returned with a few more dollars in our pockets!

When Gautam and I set off on our mission with this money, the plan was to fly to Afghanistan and then hitchhike from there to London. This route bypassed Pakistan, which didn't allow Indians to enter. There were no cellphones and no Google maps, so we relied on those now-obsolete paper ones that no one can fold. Our knapsacks were stuffed with these maps, leaving little room for anything besides our rolled-up goose-feather sleeping bags and a few clothes.

Our packs, which our dads had given us, looked impressive. They had military Indian tags stenciled on them: INDIAN AIR FORCE on his and INDIAN ARMY on mine. We had attached pins with the flags of India and the United Nations to each bag.

I felt no fear or trepidation, just adrenaline-filled excitement and pride that we had already gotten as far as the airport. If I had known what dangers lay ahead, I would have been terrified.

The beginning of our trip promised all good things. We set off on a Royal Afghani eighteen-seat propeller plane from Amritsar in India, bound for Kabul, Afghanistan. We were served bread with butter! *Life is good*, I thought. At least for now.

We *thought* our destination would be Kabul, Afghanistan, where we'd start hitchhiking. But the plane was actually going to stop at another Afghan city, Kandahar. When we landed in Kandahar, the airline officials said whoever was getting off there should simply pick up their bags and go. There was a bus you could catch to the office of Royal Afghan Airways in the city. Those who wanted to go to Kabul were instructed to stay on the plane. I looked at Gautam expectantly, and we nodded in agreement; yes, we'd deplane. This would save us a day or two of hitchhiking. So our good fortune extended beyond the treat of bread with butter.

Afghanistan was (and still is) a troubled country. It's controlled by factions of warlords and is chaotic and unstructured; nothing has changed in a thousand years. There's no economic system, just people trying to survive. There was a road going southwest out of Kandahar to Herat, a city not far from the Iranian border. The Russians had built the road from Kandahar to Kabul and northward using blacktop, while the Americans had constructed a concrete road to Herat and southwestward. We were told that there was a truck stop where the surfaces met and that riding with truckers was the only way to get anywhere by hitchhiking. The truck stop was our first destination.

I spoke in Hindi to the first Indian-looking person I saw, asking for directions to the stop. His response startled me. He advised us to take the Indian and UN flag pins off our knapsacks. "You're in Kandahar," he warned, "in an Islamic country. Be careful." *You've got to be kidding*, I thought. We already stood out as vulnerable, foreign, long-haired college kids. I asked Gautam, only half-joking if he wanted to take the next flight back.

The Indian made me so nervous that I rethought our plan to walk to the truck stop and hitchhike from there. Maybe taking a bus would be wiser. I told the man that we had some Indian rupees to pay for a bus ticket and asked if he could help. He said our money was no good in Kandahar but that he might be able to exchange it for some local currency. We were faced with a choice: Should we trust this stranger, or would he take our money and run? Would he cheat us since we didn't have any idea of the exchange rate? What should we do? Having no other choice, we instinctually decided to trust him.

The exchange rate turned out to be a twenty-three percent difference in our favor; our 100 worth of rupees netted 123 worth of Afghanis. We gave him the rupees and took the Afghani money from him. He suggested we take a bus, but we didn't want to spend any money, so he gave us directions, telling us it would be a three- or four-mile walk to the road where blacktop met concrete. Truckers could pick us up there.

We soldiered on. And quickly became lost. The roads kept turning in different directions, and there were no signs to guide us. We walked, and walked, and walked some more. Unused to carrying heavy backpacks, we were already exhausted, dirty, and hungry. As we dragged our achy, tired bodies along the dirt road, it seemed like every time we turned a corner, dust was kicking up.

We discovered the source. Three Afghanis were following us!

Rounding another turn, we were face-to-face with the men. My heart was pounding so hard I thought it would shoot straight through my chest. I had a Nepalese Gurkha knife in my backpack, but it would be impossible to reach it. And who knew if I'd even dare to use it?

Despite the fight-or-flight instinct, I was frozen and unable to act. The men spoke a language I didn't understand, not English or Hindi, maybe Pashto. It didn't matter. Their body language was clear enough; they wanted our money.

Then, one of the guys pulled out a knife!

I assessed where they were standing and what was in their hands. The knife was in the right hand of the guy closest to me, a few feet away. His two friends were just standing there with threatening expressions. They didn't have knives, not that I could see. Despite my terror, I clearly remember they were wearing cream-colored robes down to their knees with nothing underneath and sandals on their callused feet. Maybe if we ran, our sneakers could outrun their sandals.

The guy with the knife suddenly got closer to me. In a flash, I turned and swung my knapsack off my shoulder with one hand and flipped it around, hitting the guy holding the knife square in the face, hard. And finally, the survival flight instinct propelled me, and I ran, with Gautam following close behind.

I had no idea if we were running toward more danger, and my mind raced along with my body. Would our attackers ambush us ahead? Would there be more attackers? Would there be any people around who could help? Would I have the stamina to keep running?

We ran as fast and hard as we could. The young men chased us, shouting and screaming. We couldn't hear what they were saying, but we wouldn't understand them even if we could. Surprisingly, the guy I'd hit didn't drop to the ground. I wasn't able to knock him out, but I did hit him hard enough to stun him and get us a crucial five- or ten-second head start. When we got to the main road, we finally looked back. The thugs had given up and stopped chasing us. My relief was so intense that I broke down crying.

Gautam and I didn't speak for a while. We didn't know where we were. We didn't know what to do. But we made a potentially life-saving decision, no more directionless walking looking for changes in the road surface.

It was time to find a bus in this remote Afghan desert. After a bit, we got our bearings and headed back to the busy area where we'd started out. There, we saw the guy who had changed our money for us. We breathlessly told him what had happened. He just looked at us and said, "I *told* you! Take an early morning bus!" With his help, we bought tickets to get us into Iran.

The bus ride was bumpy and stomach-churning, but we were making progress on our journey to London. It was extremely crowded, and we got some strange looks from other passengers. We were so afraid of losing our knapsacks that we either sat on them or held them on our laps.

After several hours, one of our stops was at an oasis where everyone, including us, got off. It was a welcome sight in the middle of a vast desert and crumbling, rocky land. Imagine our surprise to see happy, seemingly carefree kids playing and shouting greetings to us. Here they were, in the middle of nowhere, excited to see foreign-looking strangers going through their tiny village. What a contrast from the hoodlums we had encountered earlier in Kandahar! At the oasis, I learned a very important lesson: happiness is all about your attitude and expectations.

When we arrived near Herat, our bus stopped at the border of Afghanistan and Iran. There were queues of people winding through stanchions like you see in banks or airports, except these were made of somewhat intimidating metal pipes. We showed our passports, and finally, we were in Iran.

Now, our plan to thumb our way across continents really kicked in. We hitched a ride to Mashhad in a small, primitive truck, more like a tractor, with two wheels in the front and two in the back. Surprisingly, there were some wide, six-lane roads in Mashhad that were nothing like the dirt of Kandahar.

By evening, we started to walk again. During our journey, we walked about ten hours a day on average. As it was getting dark, a taxi driver slowed to ask where we were going. When we said Teheran, he told us we were crazy. He informed us that there were exceedingly steep, rocky mountains between Mashhad and Teheran that would be almost impossible for us to traverse. The driver offered us a ride in his taxi to his home for the night.

Although tempting, the offer was somewhat frightening, and we hesitated. We had already been threatened by Afghanis, so what if this Iranian guy tried to kill us too? But my gut instinct made a split-second decision: we'd accept the ride.

I was once again questioning the wisdom of our hitchhiking plan but was reassured to hear the muezzin's call to prayer on a loudspeaker as we approached a religious Muslim town. And it was even more reassuring when the driver invited us to stay overnight in his mud house. He led us to the top of the structure and exhausted, we rolled out our sleeping bags. For the first time since we'd left India, we slept comfortably in the open air.

In the morning, our new friend served us tea and a traditional Iranian meal with meat. We were famished and sat on the floor around a large circular metal plate that everyone ate from with their hands. It was a truly wonderful communal experience. The Iranians we met later were similarly friendly and hospitable.

Our friend then drove us to a truck stop, and we thanked him profusely and tried to explain why we couldn't pay for the taxi ride. He smiled and hugged us, and kindly introduced us to truck drivers at the tea stall. All these truck stops have tea stalls, and about six people were sitting on the ground drinking tea from tiny cups when we got there. They insisted we join them for a cup, offering it like a special gift to us.

One of the truck drivers volunteered to take us to Teheran, and the ride confirmed what we had already been told: it was, indeed, a very long, rocky drive through enormous, steep mountains, so steep that the truck struggled to climb up at ten miles per hour. Even though we had slept the previous night, we were still exhausted and slept most of the way. This ride took us to the outskirts of Teheran.

We walked at least ten miles from the outskirts, searching for the *gurdwara*, a Sikh temple. It would provide a much-needed respite for us. These temples offered all travelers not only a place to pray but also to sleep and eat. (We weren't carrying any food in our backpacks, just vitamins provided by my uncle.) In the meantime, we met some very friendly Iranians who allowed us to take pictures with them. I even saw my first color TV through the window of a house! I had traveled from the prehistoric stone age in Afghanistan to the 20th century in Iran, which, at that time, was even more advanced than India.

When we finally arrived in front of a Sikh temple, I dropped to my knees and kissed the ground in gratitude. I was safe and felt at home for the first time since I left my birthplace.

A double door served as the entrance to the Sikh *gurdwara,* and inside was a hall spread with beautiful Iranian carpets. We put our knapsacks down, took off our shoes, rinsed our hands, walked in, and bowed. A priest was sitting on the floor, and he gave us parshad, which is a protein mixed with wheat, butter, and sugar. This treat is meant to revive the spirit and the body with much-needed energy. Sikhism is a way of life with a central tenet of living in truth and love, standing up for what is right, and giving to others. I certainly felt its embrace here in this temple.

I was overwhelmed and grateful as I thought about Guru Nanak, the Sikh religious leader who had traveled on foot all over the Far East, Middle East, and Central Asia, from north to south and east India, Iran, Saudi Arabia, Iraq, Kazakhstan, China, and Tibet. He returned home after walking over 28,000 kilometers, promoting peace, equality, and respect for all. I had just made a small journey on foot to safety. In my own little way, I was following in the footsteps of my religious tradition. I was at peace.

Chapter 3

TEHERAN TO TABRIZ TO TURKEY

Who would have thought that our meeting with Prime Minister Indira Gandhi in Delhi would lead us to a meeting with prominent businessmen in Teheran? Or that the hug from the prime minister would be a prelude to their handshakes?

The interim step leading to the business meeting occurred at the Indian Embassy in Teheran. After a restful night at the Sikh temple, Gautam and I walked around the city, and I was struck by how developed and westernized it was. The women wore skirts, not burkas, and the roads had cars, not pedestrians. Teheran at that time (the Shah of Iran days) seemed so advanced that I felt as if I was already in Europe. Gautam and I walked purposefully to the Indian Embassy, unencumbered by our knapsacks.

We met the military attaché, who happened to be acquainted with my dad, which was an encouraging coincidence. In conversation, I informed him of my affiliation with Rotary International, a service organization with the mission of effecting positive change globally through a network of community leaders, businesspeople, professionals, and even kids like me. Their motto is "Service Above Self," which was somewhat ironic since the Rotarians were instrumental in helping me achieve my *personal* mission to travel across continents.

The attaché had unexpectedly good news for us. He had once been a guest speaker for the Rotaractors, and they were meeting right now at the Royal Teheran Hilton Hotel. He immediately picked up the phone and asked his contact if he could send over two young Indian Rotarian guys to talk with the group. We couldn't believe we had traveled from the dirt roads of Kandahar to a glass-and-steel luxury hotel!

Gautam and I wasted no time removing our UN and Indian flag pins from our knapsacks to wear proudly on our chests. Outfitted in a relatively clean checkered shirt, jeans, and comfortable suede shoes, I rode up five floors in a modern elevator and went into an equally modern conference room with an expansive view of the highway below. The room was set up like a boardroom, with a large oval-shaped table seating about twenty-five people. Everyone looked very businesslike and official in their sharply tailored western suits and ties.

Never shy, I spoke on behalf of Gautam and myself, introducing us as the Rotarians referred by the military attaché at the Indian Embassy. We were asked to wait until their regular meeting concluded. That gave me some time to calm my nerves before one businessman asked me to explain why we were there. This was the first time I'd ever spoken to businesspeople outside of India (it would be the first of countless times during my career). Remember, I was just a college kid with long hair tied in a bandana and not-so-clean jeans. But I'd spoken to Prime Minister Gandhi, so this should be a piece of cake. I was rarely at a loss for words.

I delivered a passionate account of how I attended nine different schools, meeting westerners who knew nothing about other cultures. I explained my long involvement with Rotary International in India and described how I thought we could promote mutual understanding to achieve world peace by traveling throughout Central Asia and Europe.

Then I made eye contact with each individual at the conference table and got to the bottom line: we needed money to accomplish our objective. I launched into a colorful description of our recent adventures in Kandahar, Mashhad, and the gurdwara in Teheran. With compelling honesty, I shared how impressed and appreciative we were of the kindness and hospitality we'd received in Iran.

After my talk, we were told to wait in the conference room. I wasn't sure what to think when an imposing gentleman joined us. He asked detailed questions about our plans. I knew he was more than satisfied with my answers when he said, "what you young men are doing is exceptional, and I want to help." The businessman continued, "I own an international bus line that travels daily across the border from Tabriz to Istanbul. I will contribute to your admirable efforts by giving you two tickets for our luxury bus." He gave us a handwritten letter to exchange for tickets at the bus station. He kindly instructed us to call him if we ran into any trouble. We thanked him profusely, and I must say, I was pleased with my poise under pressure, the outcome I achieved, and the safety net he offered.

Everyone at the meeting stood up, walked over to us, and shook our hands. That was a culture shock. This behavior would have been highly unusual in the hierarchical society of India. You simply didn't shake hands with your superiors or elders; in fact, you'd deferentially call them "sir." After leaving the hotel, Gautam and I gave each other high fives. With my adrenaline level still high, I imagined that we were already in Istanbul, Turkey. We had already made such great progress in our adventure from India to Europe.

Hugs and handshakes, these were auspicious moments in my life that I'll always remember. They presaged more unbelievable opportunities, and the respect accorded me by adults gave me added confidence in my ability to achieve whatever I set out to do.

Tabriz is located on the eastern side of the Turkish-Iranian border, so all we'd need to do was get there from Teheran. We spent a couple of days sightseeing in Teheran before hitchhiking to Tabriz with our precious bus tickets to Istanbul in our pockets. We were told that visiting the marketplace would give us a clear picture of Iranian life, and indeed, it did.

The market differed from the underground one in Calcutta, and everyone was friendly and welcoming. It sold similar basic goods, including food, spices, crafts, and clothing, but it was on street level. The stalls on both sides were covered by tarps held up by poles to protect them from rain. Even though the goods were cheap, we didn't buy anything there. Our attitude was to focus, focus, focus. We had a mission and wouldn't waste money on frivolities.

Our immediate destination was the bus station in Tabriz, and we started hitchhiking again. By now, we had learned not to stick out our thumbs and expect cars to stop. Like in Iran, you found rides by going to truck stops where truckers would rest, get gas, or buy cheap tea. So, we walked about ten miles to the nearest stop. It wasn't difficult to find two rides to take us the 400 miles or so to Tabriz.

At the bus station, we effortlessly exchanged the business owner's handwritten letter for two tickets to Istanbul and were told the next bus would leave in about six hours. We wandered around for a bit and drank tea to assuage our hunger. As we relaxed, we noticed the price printed on our tickets: $25 (US dollars) each.

That's when I made my first international business deal. Gautam and I agreed to return to the bus ticket counter to see if we could exchange the tickets for cash. We felt confident that our donor would approve of our enterprising transaction. Not only did we receive a refund, but we were also asked what type of currency we wanted, Iranian rials or Turkish lira. We gratefully accepted the lira and now had a net total of $150 in value, fifty percent greater than what we had started with in the form of Afghan, Indian, and US money!

The next leg of our hitchhiking journey was upon us along a slightly hilly, dusty road in the barren desert from Iran to Turkey. Again, it wasn't difficult to find truckers. However, we got an unsettling warning from some other hitchhikers we met who were traveling in the other direction from west to east. "Be careful," we were told, "truckers are known to rape their unsuspecting passengers." One hitchhiker told us a terrifying story about one such incident.

We hadn't heeded a warning of danger back in Afghanistan, and this was more frightening news. Once again, we rethought our plan. Maybe we should try to use our recently acquired cash for bus tickets. But with the invincibility of youth and the dogged pursuit of our objective, we rationalized we'd be OK. We were traveling together, and that would serve as protection. We'd take the risk for the fifty percent additional funds in our pockets.

The truckers had a system. There were usually three men in a truck, the driver and co-driver in the front and a third person in the back assigned to help with problems like flat tires. The hitchhikers typically sat in the back or on top of the cabin, so that's where we rode most of the time.

Our first driver on the three-day journey was heading to Ankara, not Istanbul, but the route followed the same straight line until diverging to the north for Ankara and straight ahead to Istanbul. Like all our drivers, the guy didn't speak English, but we communicated through a mix of universal sign language and maps. The driver seemed to understand that we were earnest, young kids, and we hoped to convey a good feeling about the UN, India, and the prospect of world peace.

I didn't think anything could surpass the excitement of my driving adventures in my father's military Jeep, but the thrill of riding on top of a lorry across macadam-topped roads with the wind roaring powerfully was amazing. And, oh, the bumps! We were going less than forty miles per hour, but without shock absorbers, every bump jolted my body. I loved it, but I wasn't quite daring enough to jump on top while the truck was moving like I saw one guy do. Today, I drive a Porsche 911, which reminds me fondly of those bumpy rides.

The view from the top of the truck was desert-like. There was no vegetation and just wide-open barrenness. Now and again, we'd see a small oasis dotted with little villages and palm trees. We didn't leave the truck when we stopped at villages. Even though we had money belts containing our cash and passports hidden under our shirts, we were afraid to abandon our few supplies. Sitting on top of a truck wasn't conducive to sleep, so we stayed awake for the duration of this ride. Plus, the novelty and excitement of the trip kept us awake.

Gautam and I became familiar with the truckers' routines. They drove day and night, only stopping every two to three hours. Streams became our baths and toilets. It was a long, long trip to Ankara, comprising 1,200 miles in just a few days. We were thrilled to be that much closer to our destination.

When we got a new ride near Ankara heading towards Istanbul, we had our first opportunity to sleep. There were two drivers, and a young kid about our age didn't mind watching our stuff when we stopped in a little village. We hesitated to close our eyes, but exhaustion overpowered us. After our snooze, we didn't feel especially rested, but we had been primed for all-nighters as college kids.

This ride took us to the Asian side of Istanbul, where there was an area where truckers stopped for clearance to transport their goods. The stop was just before the Bosphorus, also known as the Strait of Istanbul, the continental divide between Asia and Europe in northwestern Turkey. There is a one-mile suspension bridge spanning the strait. At that time, the bridge was open to pedestrian traffic. Guess how we got to Istanbul?

What an unbelievable feeling it was to walk across the Bosphorus. We could actually see Europe. Gautam and I stood on the bridge feeling victorious.

I also felt like I was traveling in time toward modernity. Tehran was more developed than Delhi, and Istanbul was more developed than Tehran. From there, the degrees of advancement spiraled exponentially throughout the European cities we visited.

Our sleeping accommodations improved as well. Istanbul was the first place where we stayed in a youth hostel. The maps we had stuffed in our knapsacks in India, seemingly a very long time ago, indicated two essential landmarks: youth hostels and post offices. The youth hostel in Istanbul housed at least twenty kids in a room, one on top of the other. The bathroom was filthy dirty, and stank, but there was running water and soap. Everything is relative, and this was an improvement on an open-air toilet. And the $2.00 a night we splurged on the hostel was worth it.

The only way I could communicate with my parents at home was via self-sealing aerograms made of delicately thin paper. I had mailed one to my dad in Teheran and was extremely pleased to find one from him waiting for me at the main post office in Istanbul. It was written in his typically terse, upbeat style and was most welcome.

You can't be in Istanbul without visiting the Grand Mosque, and it was as impressive as I'd expected. We also went to the market, which was surprisingly elegant. The degrees of modernity of the bazaars I visited, like the accommodations, continued to increase progressively.

Throughout our trip, other hitchhikers were a great source of information. We learned that going through Greece and crossing the Adriatic Sea via Greece to Italy was the best route from Istanbul. The land routes weren't advisable because they traveled through communist countries. After spending a few days in Istanbul, we headed to the railway station with a plan to go to Athens through Thessaloniki and then to Ioannina from Athens.

The railway station was unlike any I'd seen so far. It was a big complex with trains from all over Europe. The cheapest ticket was for a local train. Our first stop was a small town in the suburbs of Istanbul, and we had a terrific experience there. We met a young Turkish guy who commuted from there to Istanbul. He asked where we were going and then explained that there were no long-distance trains to our destination. He graciously invited us to spend the night at his apartment. The encounter was another example of the hospitality we received on our trip. The people we met were as important and memorable, if not more so than the places we saw.

The apartment was in a five-story building with no elevator, and we slept in the young man's carpeted living room, which felt truly luxurious. He spoke in broken English, but we easily found ways to communicate that transcended language. Without words or intentionality, we were, indeed, promoting mutual understanding between different cultures. The guy helped plan our itinerary on a map, and we used our lira to buy train tickets to Thessaloniki instead of hitchhiking.

It was late in the evening when we got off the train. It was very dark, and everything was closed. Exhausted, we plopped our sleeping bags on the pavement and slept with our backpacks safely stowed underneath our bodies. We didn't realize that we were lying on a major walkway to and from the train station until the morning when we felt people jumping over us.

After a slice of bread and a glass of milk, we got on our way, hitching to Athens. We could have taken a train, but we were committed to frugality. And we were so determined to reach our destination in London that we didn't sightsee much in Athens. That would have to wait for another trip when I was older. We saw the Parthenon and other ruins from afar but quickly pressed onward.

From Athens, we hitchhiked to Ioannina in northwestern Greece. The beauty and calm of the Adriatic Sea were spectacular. As soon as we were on its shores, we stripped off our knapsacks and clothes and jumped in for a refreshing, cleansing swim. Swimming in the Adriatic Sea was like swimming in a calm, clear lake. It was a thrilling feeling I'll never forget.

Chapter 4

FROM THE VATICAN TO A PARISIAN JAIL

Our plan now was to travel through Italy, and the best route from Ioannina was to take a large ferry to Bari, with a stopover in Corfu. I spent $10 of my $100 dollars to buy the boat ticket. We wanted to save our drachmas and lira for the trip home. The purchase transaction was memorable because I used a traveler's check for the first time. It was hard to imagine that a piece of paper with my name on it was worth money. I took my authority to sign a check in exchange for a ticket seriously and dutifully recorded the date and serial number in the check register. Little did I know that later in life, signing checks would not be fun at all.

Corfu comprises rugged mountains and has several lively, luxurious resorts studding the shoreline. For me, it offered the paradise of partying. I met many Canadians and was invited to a party on the top of the Corfu ridge. The atmosphere was so festive it reminded me of an Indian wedding with music, dancing, and drinking. Beer and other alcohol flowed freely. Apparently, Greek traditions aren't so different from Indian ones. I'd had alcohol before, but this was the first time I got really drunk. This is yet another of the many, many "firsts" I experienced during my youthful travels.

Some time before, I had bought a book on palmistry on a whim because the subject seemed intriguing. Well, it turned out to be quite useful here on this Greek resort island. I started to talk to a girl at the party about reading palms, and the next thing I knew, I was touted as an expert. Kids sought me out to read their palms in exchange for beers! It was also a sly way to get to hold a girl's hand.

Gautam and I slept fitfully up on the hill that night. After waking up late in the afternoon, we took a short boat ride to the town of Bari in Italy. From there, on our way to Rome, we went to Brindisi on the west coast of the Adriatic Sea on our way to Rome. This was the first time cars actually picked us up instead of truck drivers and the first time we got rides from families.

We learned from our Canadian friends in Corfu it was best to hitch rides at rest areas on the highways where people stopped for gas. They warned that Italian cops were tough, and we risked getting picked up by them on the road. We heeded our new friends' advice and practiced what to say to the folk at the rest areas. It turned out that girls were more likely than guys to give us rides. We didn't mind.

We ended up on a little hill near the road circling the City of Rome and found a picnic area where we met a nice Italian couple relaxing. They offered us drinks and ham sandwiches, a novel food that I got used to eating in Europe. The couple also gave us a bottle of wine, which we didn't finish; we'd had plenty of alcohol in Corfu.

The next morning, we hitched a ride into Rome, still carrying the rest of that bottle of wine. When we got to the Vatican, there was a sign: "No alcohol allowed." We walked in with our bottle hidden under our shirts anyway. We weren't going to waste it, but we did feel guilty. I remember thinking, "We're going to get punished for this! We're walking into a holy place!" The Vatican was magnificent, and we prayed for forgiveness for bringing that wine bottle in when we left that evening.

We walked around Rome, and I was awed by the architecture, the fountains, all the history, and even the wide roads. I felt like my jaw was constantly dropping in amazement. We didn't buy tickets to any attractions and lived on milk, bread, and vitamins, spending less than $2 a day per person. We were basically fasting, yet it was incredible how much energy we had.

After Rome, we hitched to Milan, stopping in Florence along the way. Our time in Florence was one of the few disappointments on my trip. A professor from our university in Banares was living there on sabbatical, and I looked forward to the familiarity of an Indian face. We spent about three-quarters of a day searching for his house and were astounded when he didn't open the door for us. How could someone from our university, from our country, not extend the bare minimum of hospitality by acknowledging our presence? Strangers from all over the world had opened their homes and their tables to us, but not a compatriot.

From Florence, we went to Milan and hitchhiked across the Alps to our next destination, Zurich. The feeling of being in the Alps was almost indescribable; the mountains' sheer steepness and natural beauty were overwhelming. When we got to Zurich, we still had a short way to go to town but were so exhausted that we spent a night under an overpass. It was actually very comfortable.

We reached Zurich mid-morning and soon found ourselves in a local park. Zurich was immaculate, except for this one area known to be a hangout for drug addicts. That's precisely where we had stumbled upon. Not until we saw needles lying around did we realize that we had to go elsewhere.

The next day, we contacted the parents of a Swiss girl we'd met at Banaras Hindu University who was heading to Australia with her boyfriend. They were wonderful people. We stayed at their house for about three days, and they took us around the museums. It was a blessing to be able to clean up at their house, wash our hair, and have some good meals for three consecutive days. After that, we went to Geneva and then hitchhiked to Paris. Without any doubt, Switzerland is the most beautiful country I have ever visited.

Our ride dropped us off in the evening on the outskirts of Paris, and we took a train straight to the beautiful Gare du Nord station. There were offices on the second floor of the train station, and Gautam and I were just so exhausted that we stretched our sleeping bags out on the floor of one of these offices, and off we went to sleep.

The next thing I knew, a huge German Shepherd dog was about six inches away from my face, barking hungrily. A tall guy was holding the leash.

It was the French police.

The cops were shouting at us, and their dogs were barking, but we couldn't speak French, and they couldn't speak English. What they were saying, of course, was that we were trespassing. They put us into a police van, blared the siren, and took off. We had no idea where we were going or what their intentions were. In my naïveté, I thought maybe they were trying to help us. Jail was the furthest thing from my mind.

Now here's another first I experienced on this trip: a night in jail.

The jail's superintendent was a man in his forties from Africa's Ivory Coast. He was a very tough guy and completely bald. In broken English, he asked us what had happened. We explained our peace mission and told him we were military officers' children, and please, please, we needed to get to the Indian Embassy. The cop was sympathetic. I think he'd had a tough time coming to France and understood what it was like to be and look different.

He apologized to us, saying that it was unfair we had been arrested. Unfair that people like us who were trying to do good were misunderstood. And he felt so badly jailing us that he left the doors to our cells open. That way, he explained, we wouldn't feel too afraid. It was a city jail, but nobody was in any of the half-dozen or so tiny cells that day, so he gave us separate cells. He assured us that we'd be taken to the Indian Embassy in the morning. Despite the cold concrete floor, we slept pretty well.

I'll never forget the superintendent's compassion. The only thing was he was required to keep our passports while we were in jail.

When we got up in the morning, the cop from the Ivory Coast had left a note for us. Now we just wanted to get our passports back. We didn't care about anything else. The new cop on duty was French and didn't speak much English and seemed to have difficulty locating our passports. We were still scared; what if they charged us for trespassing or something more serious? But he found our passports, gave them back, and then put us into a police car to be taken to the Indian embassy.

At the Indian embassy, we were brought to the military attaché for the government of India. And wouldn't you know it, the military attaché just happened to have a friend in common with my dad! It's such a small world.

We learned that the cop from the Ivory Coast had done us another kindness the previous night. He had contacted the Indian Embassy to verify our story and make them aware of our situation. When we arrived at the embassy, everything was already sorted out. The officials wanted me to try to reach my dad, but he was stationed at a post in the mountains in Northeast India, and I couldn't reach him. Nevertheless, the embassy took care of everything, and we spent a pleasant day walking around Paris.

Throughout the trip, we would buy small postcards from every major city we visited and send them to our parents in India to keep them up to date. France was the first place where we sat down and wrote on official Indian Government stationery. We were selective about what we told our parents. The letters said, essentially, "Hi Mom and Dad, we're fine, we still have our money and are having a great time. We're in Paris, at the embassy. Nothing to worry about. It's all great—no incidents!"

We took the train from Paris to Calais and then got in line to take the ferry to Dover on the English coast. The British Immigration and Customs officers in Calais were very tough. They grilled us at length. Why were we going to London? Where were our tickets? Where were our passports? How would we get back home with the little money we had? How long were we planning to be in London? Where were we going to stay?

We told them we had some family friends in Coventry (my distant cousin lived there), and Gautam had family friends in London. We had no problem anywhere else because we had got all our visas in Delhi. In contrast, these customs officers gave us a very hard time.

We missed our first boat. There were others every two hours or so, but this was starting to look serious. We feared the guard wouldn't let us into England. We showed him all our government letters and passports; we had dual entry visas to go in and out of many countries we visited, including the other European countries. However, we didn't have all the necessary visas that would get us back to India, and we had no money to get back unless we traveled overland. The British guard said, essentially, "You're going to have to go back to India."

Gautam bravely suggested they call the military attaché in Paris. After about two hours of interrogation and endless back-and-forth, we *finally* got through, but the guard stamped on our passports, "Entry restricted to 30 days." He said that if we stayed longer than thirty days, we'd go to jail. Again.

We had a very rough crossing by boat across the English Channel in a storm. When we got to the English shore, we took a connecting train from Dover to London's Waterloo Station and from there to a place called Southhall, where my family friends lived. They were Indian, so we were treated to home-cooked Indian meals for the first time on our trip. For an eighteen-year-old kid, the familiar food was very comforting and delicious. It certainly made up for all the previous days of subsisting on bread and vitamins.

We stayed in London for a few days, did some sightseeing, and then went to our appointment at the Indian High Commissioner's office near Trafalgar Square (in other countries, the person who holds that position is called an ambassador, but in Britain, they are called the high commissioner). We showed them our letter from Mrs. Gandhi's office and were served a traditional English tea with biscuits with the high commissioner at a long table. The tea service was made of fine bone china with the Indian flag emblazoned on the cups. I felt a swell of pride and talked about our mission to promote understanding of India and its culture to youth around the world. To raise awareness of what unites us.

The high commissioner was impressed by our efforts, and he did something we weren't expecting. He called the BBC and told them about these two Indian kids who had been hitchhiking around Asia and Europe to promote peace and international understanding. Before we knew it, he had arranged for his attaché to take us to BBC studios. After we arrived, a reporter took us to London Bridge and interviewed us for BBC Radio. They took a picture of us on the bridge and wrote up a story to go along with the radio interview.

Standing on top of London Bridge talking to reporters, I felt like I had reached the peak of Mount Everest. Along the way, I faced many obstacles and emerged triumphant.

I was becoming increasingly comfortable with public speaking, but my nerves were jangling when the interviewer thrust a microphone in my face. I was asked detailed questions about our trip and mission. I was exuberantly positive and avoided any mention of our unpleasant encounters. The interview experience was valuable preparation for the frequent presentations I'd make throughout my career. It reassured me that I was capable of speaking cogently and extemporaneously. To this day, I speak without notes or a written script. As I did atop London Bridge, I speak from the heart.

BBC Radio was broadcast at night in India as BBC International. The Indian High Commissioner sent a telegram to our parents for us, telling them Gautam and I were going to be on BBC Radio. They released this story to the Indian press and told our parents to look out for it, as there was a chance the story might be carried in the Indian newspaper with our photographs. Sure enough, our picture appeared in several newspapers, including the *Tribune,* which my parents read each day, with the Tower of London and the Thames River in the background.

Two weeks later, I received a postcard from my mom, expressing her pride in my accomplishments. She added that it was time for me to come home. Nevertheless, the postcard was an incredibly meaningful affirmation from her since she had been vehemently opposed to my taking the trip. My mom saved the newspaper clipping. I wish I knew where it was now.

From London, my base for about two weeks became Leicester, about two hours northwest, where I stayed with a distant cousin. It was a time to relax and recharge my batteries. After subsisting on bread, tea, and milk, it was a treat to continue with home-cooked meals. A real bed, a roof over my head, and showers were all luxuries compared to the conditions of hitchhiking. It was also wonderful to be taken sightseeing in my host's car instead of hitchhiking. We visited the usual tourist attractions, including Stratford-on-Avon, Oxford, and Cambridge.

By far, the most impressive sight was Stonehenge. Those massive megalithic stones arranged symmetrically were simply awe-inspiring. Not for the first time on my journey, I felt a deep spiritual connection.

Chapter 5

THE WAY HOME: BUYING A GUN IN KABUL

Mission accomplished! Objectives achieved! Gautam and I had introduced ourselves – two Indian youths who believed world peace is possible through mutual understanding – to western Europeans. We also had a blast traveling and exploring new places, people, and cultures. I wish I could say we also tasted new cuisines, but our lack of money kept us mainly subsisting on bread, milk, and vitamins. Let me take you on our journey back home to India from London on planes, buses, trains, foot, and by hitchhiking.

Besides the varied modes of transportation, our experiences and encounters were studies in contrasts. The red-light district in Amsterdam and Anne Frank's house. The Star-Club in Hamburg, where the young Beatles played in the early 60s, and Lubeck, Germany, with its medieval brick architecture. Passing through communist countries on the Orient Express train. These are just a few of the highlights, so I'll begin at the beginning with our $10 flight from London to Brussels.

Youth hostels weren't only a place to crash at night in Europe, but they were also a good source of traveling information for kids like us. We saw a post on a bulletin board for a cheap student flight to Brussels and Amsterdam, and off we went. When we landed at the Brussels airport, there was a free shuttle bus to Amsterdam, so we wasted no time taking advantage of it rather than hanging out in Brussels. The bus took us to Amsterdam's central bus station, a beautiful introduction to a beautiful city nicknamed the Venice of the North for its canals.

Somehow, we ended up in the red-light district. That was certainly an eye-opening experience for a college-aged kid from India! Barely clad women sitting in windows and yelling out to passersby. What are they selling, I wondered, bras, or clothing, or…? I had been shocked in Teheran when I saw girls wearing miniskirts in an Islamic country, but this was something else entirely.

This view of vibrant city life was a sharp contrast to our next stop in Amsterdam: Anne Frank's house. I had really wanted to visit, as I had read her book at my private school in India and had been fascinated. We studied European history and literature at my high school. I had learned about the Nazi's destruction of Jewish families, and Anne Frank's story felt deeply personal. I had even written a school essay about her determination in the face of genocide.

We spent the night outside the train station in Amsterdam and took a local train toward the highway the following day. We had learned that being close to a highway was the best way to get a ride hitchhiking. Our next stop was Hamburg, where we got another glimpse of western culture. There was a tunnel under the river into the old part of the city where we found many bars. Of course, we couldn't afford to drink, but we did soak up Hamburg's history. For us, The Fab Four had the starring role.

The Beatles got their start in the 1960s performing at the Star Club in Hamburg, and they'd hang out at the local bars. The area looked somewhat rundown and even dangerous, more so since we were vulnerable kids with all our valuables in knapsacks, but excitement won over fear. At the bars, we heard stories about the Beatles, like Paul McCartney's propensity to run up a tab, get drunk, and walk out without paying. Although I was more of a Rolling Stones fan and even wore a Mick Jagger-style belt, I thoroughly enjoyed hearing local insiders' tales about the Beatles.

Gautam and I met two very nice ladies in their 40s who were fascinated by us. They told us they were headed to Copenhagen and offered us a ride in their Volkswagen. We hadn't planned on visiting Copenhagen (our objective was to go to Frankfurt and on to Munich), but how could we pass up this opportunity? Rides like these made me feel like our goal of international understanding was mutual, as we East Asians learned about the kindness of Europeans throughout our trip.

Our volunteer tour guides wanted to stop in Lubeck, which is close to the

German and Danish border, and I ended up being grateful for this unplanned detour because the architecture was striking. I was particularly impressed by the imposing gothic brick architecture epitomized by its entrance gate. The city center is now a UNESCO World Heritage Site. The kind ladies dropped us off at a youth hostel in Copenhagen, where we met lots of students who were into music, playing guitar, and singing.

In addition to gaining entertainment and camaraderie, we profited from the kids in another way. I made $18 reading palms.

When I was a student at Delhi Public School, I picked up a cheap little paperback book on palmistry from a street stall in Connaught Place in Delhi and had been intrigued. Banaras Hindu University offered classes in palmistry and astrology because it considered them to be sciences. As a business student, I couldn't take those courses; instead, my friends and I practiced reading each other's palms. The basics were easy to master, identifying the lifeline, heart line, and head line. And you can tell a lot about a person's personality by just touching their hands. Right off the bat, you're "right" fifty percent of the time, and as you gain experience, your odds go higher.

I had practiced my palm reading skills in Corfu, mostly with Canadian girls. Guys couldn't care less about this stuff, but some girls would insist their boyfriends get their palms read. I guess the girls hoped to find out if they'd get married. Westerners were intrigued by us brown-skinned foreigners from faraway East Asia and intrigued by our fortune-telling skills. Our ability to speak English was valuable, and when we introduced ourselves throughout our trip, we always described our mission. The stickers we got in each country and put on our knapsacks were proud emblems of the authenticity of our purpose.

At the Copenhagen hostel, my palmistry enterprise put us $3 ahead. We had spent $15 on the way from London to Copenhagen and had just earned $18.

Our good fortune continued. We met an Indian taxi driver in this colorful city. He was astonished to meet kids from his country backpacking around and asked what on earth we were doing there, and I asked him the very same question. He showed us around some touristy spots, and when we told him about stumbling upon the red-light district in Amsterdam, he took us to one nearby. We sure were getting an education in comparative international culture, both the seemly and less seemly sides. My naïveté was evolving into worldliness.

The taxi driver made a surprisingly gracious offer to buy us train tickets back to Hamburg. Can you imagine someone who was basically a stranger buying us tickets? So once again, we benefited from a chance encounter with a kind person. We wasted no time hitchhiking from Hamburg to Hanover to Frankfurt to Munich because we were anxious to get to the Munich post office. We were expecting letters from our families there, and we weren't disappointed. Our written exchanges with our cheap postcards were always brief but heartily welcomed. Amsterdam and Hamburg were unique, but Munich was an even more picturesque city; I was particularly awed by the historic center of the town and its architecture.

At the post office, we learned about the Orient Express. Imagine, a fancy train traveling from Paris to Istanbul!

Obviously, we couldn't afford to travel in such luxury, but the train had cheap student tickets, about $4 each, for an unreserved compartment. That would save us the $12 airfare from Frankfurt to Istanbul. It also solved two other problems. We wouldn't have to hitchhike through communist countries (despite my curiosity), and we wouldn't have to rely on our contingency plan of going back by the same route we had come on. We quickly hitchhiked to Salzburg to board the train. Along the way, we went by the house where Hitler was born. Needless to say, we didn't stop there.

When we arrived at the Orient Express platform, a band was playing, and we wondered if we were in the right spot. A band welcoming people? Here? But that was the platform for the full-paying customers; ours was different. We knew the ride would be long, so we splurged on sausage sandwiches. Of course, unlike the reserved luxury train, there was no dining car in our packed compartment, and the sandwiches were our only sustenance for the duration of the ride. For six hours, we stood in the crowded compartment or, if we were lucky, sat on our knapsacks. But we were used to traveling like this on Indian trains, and we finally got seats on hard benches in Bucharest. It's amazing how comfort is relative.

Flags with the Communist symbol of a hammer and sickle were hanging everywhere. Stopping in Romania and Hungary, we had become used to policemen boarding the train, doing searches, and checking our passports. But when we got to Bulgaria in the night, we unknowingly stepped out into another level of high adventure. Outside, we came face-to-face with an armed policeman with a red armband, who ordered us to immediately get back on the train. He yelled at us with a gun, saying, "how can you dare step onto Bulgarian soil? You're only cleared to go straight to Istanbul!" The police probably thought we were Muslims, which didn't help. The Turks and Bulgarians didn't get along. We were accustomed to friendly, welcoming experiences, and this was one of the few times we felt uncomfortable, not counting our traveling conditions.

The Orient Express took about ten hours to get to Istanbul, and it stopped at a station about ten miles outside of the city. From there, we took a local train to central Istanbul and headed to the Iranian embassy because we needed visas to travel back through Iran. An Indian man was in front of us in the line, and we started to chat. He spoke Punjabi, and we had an animated conversation in our native language. He was an older man, an itinerant worker who worked in the Iranian oil fields and did odd jobs in Germany, ironic since we'd just come from there. He was shuttling a bus from Istanbul to deliver to Kabul, and we easily convinced him to give us a ride. He couldn't believe we had hitchhiked through some of the areas we did. And we couldn't believe we had a ride all the way to Kabul.

We promised the driver we'd do whatever we could to help him with the bus – change tires, whatever he needed. He traveled with an assistant, a young Afghani man, and told us to give him an address to come pick us up the next day. So, we stayed in a filthy youth hostel we were all too familiar with from the beginning of our trip, and we prayed he'd actually come back for us.

He did! The bus was one of those junky Mercedes buses from Germany, so it wasn't a luxury one like the one we had tickets for to ride from Tabriz to Istanbul. In this bus, you felt every pothole and every stone on the road. We stopped at a stream to take a little bath, another routine we'd become accustomed to, and continued onward. When we reached the fork that headed to Ankara, where we had switched rides on our way, we stopped at the same place. There were lots of hitchhikers there, and we encouraged our driver to pick some up. He was reluctant and told us he wasn't allowed, but we had been no trouble. We only had one flat tire along the way, but the Indian driver refused our offer to help fix it.

Again, comfort is relative, and despite the noise and bumps and dirt, this bus felt luxurious. We would sleep on the hard benches (better than standing up on a sardine-packed train) and stop whenever we wanted to use a bathroom (better than holding it in). It was enjoyable to share stories with our driver, a married Sikh who was originally from Delhi like us and still had family there. We told him about the beautiful Sikh gurdwara in Teheran, where we had had a welcome respite, and he stopped there even though he had intended to drive straight through. With spirits and bodies restored, we were back on the road after a night at the gurdwara.

The ride through the mountains between Teheran and Mashhad (where a seemingly long time ago, we'd naively thought we could hitchhike) was very different this time. Instead of freezing and trying to hold on to prevent jolting and falling, we enjoyed riding through the countryside and seeing it from a different perspective. When we went into Herat and Kandahar, we stopped at the same place where we had had tea months ago, the one with large groups of impoverished kids who were so happily playing and friendly. The journey from Istanbul to Kabul took about seven days, and, once again, our diet was mainly bread. When we arrived in Kabul, you'd think we would be totally depleted and exhausted, but we actually felt energized, and excitement overpowered exhaustion. Now, just thinking about this trip, I feel exhausted!

My goal in Kabul was to buy a gun.

Yes, a gun, as a gift for my father. I had bought a transistor radio for him earlier. Still, I knew as a military man and gun collector, he'd treasure a pistol. Our driver took us to a flea market in Kabul, and I bought an antique Remington for about ten dollars. Then, the driver told us about a gurdwara. This was the same one that, years later, the Taliban brutally destroyed and where they murdered a dozen Sikhs. We stopped there for two nights. This gurdwara wasn't as elaborate as the one in Teheran; it was about one-fifth the size, but it had a very, very special history.

Guru Nanak, the founder of Sikhism, visited Kabul in the early 1500s, and many Afghanis converted and settled there. Another Sikh leader, Maharaja Ranjit Singh, known as the Lion of Punjab, visited in the early 1800s when Sikhs ruled over what is now Afghanistan, Pakistan, North India, and Tibet. Here walked my forefathers! I felt an indescribable spiritual connection and still, to this day, vividly remember the feelings I had when visiting as a youth.

However, I had a conflict in this peaceful place. No one except Gautam and our driver knew I had bought a gun, but I did mention it to a local in Kabul. This man told me bluntly that I shouldn't bring it with me; it was much too dangerous. He frightened me, but there was no way I would leave the gun anywhere. It was too costly, and it was a heartfelt gift for my father. What was I going to do?

I stuck the gun inside my knapsack. Then, I opened the pack to check. And I kept checking. Then I carefully wrapped the weapon in my clothes and continued my ritual of checking. I prayed the whole way on our flight from Kabul to Amritsar, India, for fear of being caught with contraband. When we landed and went through customs, our bags were taken to be searched. I was terrified, not the feeling I expected upon returning home from a three-and-a-half-month journey of over four thousand miles.

The gun wasn't detected, and a powerful feeling of joy and triumph replaced my fear. I hadn't given up, despite the many bumps in the road, on my mission to London and back to India. It was a transformative experience that continues to impact every facet of my life.

Chapter 6

HOME IN INDIA... AND ALONE IN THE UNITED STATES

What a relief to be safely home in India! What a tremendous sense of accomplishment. And what an overwhelming honor to be welcomed back as a hero.

The pride I felt in myself rivaled the admiration I received, especially from my friends and teachers at Banaras Hindu University in Banaras (Varanasi), who affectionately nicknamed me Sid. Whenever I return to India, I'm asked about my adventures throughout Asia and Europe. Today, it's rather ordinary for a student to travel internationally and, in the act of doing so, promote cross-cultural understanding. But at the time, my experiences were extraordinary.

I arrived home in September 1969 and missed the first thirty-five days of my college classes at the beginning of the fall semester. No one, not professors or administrators or peers, was critical of my absence. I still managed to get all As. Further, the positive publicity we received from the newspaper report of my BBC interview in London helped legitimize our trip as a worthy endeavor.

I can still remember the welcome Gautam and I received at the university. The whole school gathered in the auditorium, and we were invited on stage. We enthusiastically described our hitchhiking story and adventures. As usual, I did most of the talking. We even inspired two junior-year students to do the same thing the following year.

But whenever I shared memories of my trip, I was very, very clear that this was just the start. I wasn't just looking back at my recent past; I was looking forward to an expansive, bright future. I was planning to study in the United States, make money, and make something of myself. I didn't know exactly what I'd do or where I'd live in the US, just as I didn't know exactly how I'd get to London or what I'd do there. But I was absolutely determined to live and study in America someday soon. My father's teachings inspired me to have a clear vision and make it a reality. I knew I could. I knew I wouldn't give up until I achieved my goal.

My trip had solidified what would become my overarching principle in life, to never, ever, ever give up. Not even when there are setbacks and everything looks bleak. Not even when there are successes because, with perseverance, successes will multiply.

My plan to study in America took root when I was in eighth or ninth grade. My cousin, Sher, who was about twenty years older than me, and my older brother Harry were my role models. My cousin emigrated to America and studied engineering at the University of Michigan, which has a very competitive, highly ranked engineering program. He visited my family on one of his trips back to India, and that was a pivotal moment in my thinking. I was entranced by my cousin's description of how he managed to board a ship to America and make his way to university. Later, he became a successful self-made man. At a young age, I was determined to be like him. Specifically, I was determined to follow his footsteps across oceans and create my own story of business success.

I was also inspired by my brother, who managed to reach the US to study mechanical engineering at the University of Michigan. He had no money and worked eight-plus hours a day at odd jobs like standing in front of a scorching-hot oven baking pizza while he went to school. He did whatever it took, and I would too. As I was finishing my senior year at Banaras, I studiously researched university MBA programs in the US to build upon my undergraduate business studies and fulfill my vision.

I borrowed books from the library and studied hard for the required standardized entrance exam, the Admission Test for Graduate School in Business (ATGSB), which is now called the Graduate Management Admission Test (GMAT). My score was just average, which wasn't surprising since I was never good at memorizing, or tests for that matter. Next, I scoured all the thick, encyclopedic books in the library with detailed descriptions of US universities. I identified the primary criteria for schools to maximize my chances of acceptance; schools without a stringent requirement for the ATGSB, ones that offered financial aid to international students, and smaller, less competitive schools that would be more likely to read my letter. I was realistic, but I couldn't resist applying to the Ivies as well – Penn, Columbia, and Stanford.

After compiling a list of universities, I launched my plan of attack: a letter-writing campaign.

Yes, good old-fashioned letters on cheap aerograms of tissue-thin paper with cheap postage that you folded and sealed to form a letter. I sent over forty letters! My gut told me that my admission chances were slim, even in 1971, but I was undeterred. Since my time was limited, copy machines weren't available, and I was a poor typist, I used carbon paper to type three letters at a time. My approach was systematic: the originals went to the best schools, the copies to others.

The letters were sincere. I began with a humble apology, writing it may seem odd that I was sending this request for admission without filing a formal application. However, I wrote, I can't afford the graduate school application fees. I explained that I was hard-working and resourceful. Hopefully, that was implied by the very fact of my letter. Further, I explained my unwavering passion for attending university in the United States and earn an MBA. I promised that once I was successful, I was committed to giving back my good fortune to the school and to society in appreciation of my excellent education. I made good on my promises, which you'll learn about later. I expressed my commitment to promoting international understanding. If you give me a chance, I wrote, I'll pay it forward. I also included personal information, a kind of resume that we then called biodata, about myself, my extracurricular activities, and my grades.

And then, I waited and dreamed.

Of the forty schools I wrote to, I heard back from two with admissions offers. They were Andrews University (a Seventh-Day Adventist school) in Michigan and Wilkes College (now Wilkes University) in Pennsylvania.

A five percent response rate. Not a bad return on my paltry investment in flimsy aerograms and carbon paper. There was a problem, though. Neither Andrews nor Wilkes offered me financial aid. Or so I thought.

I reread the Wilkes letter written by the dean of students, George Ralston, which had included an I-20 admission form for foreign students. And then, I saw it! The dean actually *did* say the university would award me a full scholarship and free housing in the dorm. Wow! Another good return on my investment! Wilkes asked for additional information like letters of recommendation, which I wasted no time providing. I was fortunate and grateful and convinced that my acceptance reflected the kind of country America is, a compassionate land of opportunity.

Unfortunately, there was a sad, unforeseen bump in my road to America. My dad suddenly got sick. He was hospitalized and eventually diagnosed with cancer. How could I go overseas and leave my family now? I did have a backup plan. I had also been accepted to the Punjab University MBA program, where I'd applied as a safety school. It wasn't a Harvard, it was more on the level of a UC-Berkeley, but it was well-regarded in India. My mom insisted that was the best option. She had never wanted me to leave India, and now she argued that my dad was sick, my sister was only seven, and they needed me. My mom had a pattern of giving something and then getting her way, and this time was no exception. She offered me a Vespa scooter, which was a very big deal.

I told my father about my revised plan that I would attend Punjab University. He insisted that I go to America. He recognized it was something I'd always wanted to do and told me to seize the opportunity and achieve my mission. He was unwavering in his support. With his blessing, I was on my way to the United States!

It was time to make my travel arrangements. I intended to find the cheapest flight to John F. Kennedy Airport in New York City and, from there, fly to Philadelphia. I've learned that it's helpful to ask questions, especially to people who will likely have knowledgeable answers. My roommate was C.P. Ganesh, whose father worked at the Ford Foundation, so C.P. and I went to Delhi to ask him for travel advice. He suggested Pan Am, which was the biggest airline at the time. In those days, you bought tickets at a city office, marked by a sign reading "Airlines," stood in long lines, and then were issued handwritten tickets. Quaint, by today's standards.

At the ticket counter, I asked about Pan Am's flights to the US and whether there were any even better fares. There was an inexpensive flight on Iraqi Airways. *Hey*, I thought, *I believe in peaceful international relations*, and I bought the ticket. Besides, I had flown on Royal Afghani Airways, eating only bread and butter. Comparatively, Iraqi Airways was luxurious; it would serve a meal.

Iraqi Airways flew old Boeing 707 narrow-bodied jets that could only travel a limited number of miles in one go. As a result, the trip would require multiple stops. I didn't care; I just wanted to get to my destination. It was a very long trip, from Delhi to Bagdad, then to Beirut. I took a TWA flight from Beirut to London, then a TWA flight from London to New York City. Next, I'd need to travel to Philadelphia. It was a lot of hopping around, taking almost three days, but three days is nothing when you've hitchhiked for several months, as I had.

I've never felt more excitement than when I landed in America. My previous trip hitchhiking, traveling throughout Europe, and successfully returning to India, was certainly exciting. *But this trip to America was a whole new level. It represented the possibility of a whole new life.* I was leaving my country for a new one, intent on making something of myself. I'd be there studying for a couple of years, and then, who knew what ventures would be next?

In New York, I was supposed to take a connecting flight to Philadelphia, but there was a problem. I had a ticket but no reservation on National Airlines (which is no longer around). It was nighttime, and I had no idea how far Philadelphia was from New York. Also, I didn't know what travel options were available. Thankfully, once again, I was the beneficiary of others' kindness. The airline employees gave me a seat on the stewardesses' jump seat in the back of the plane for the thirty-minute flight from New York to Philly. Every time I travel now and see those little seats by the exit,

I remember how the stewardesses were so sweet to me, a scruffy Indian kid going to college in America.

My brother was already in Philadelphia, staying with our cousin and working a summer job before his final year at the University of Michigan. When I got to Philly, my brother picked me up, and we headed to our cousin's house in Media, Pennsylvania. They had converted a walk-in closet into a bedroom, where I spent my first night in America. But I'd had much worse accommodations, and I was exhausted and grateful for a bed.

The next day, I walked to a drugstore and made my first purchase in my new country, a pair of elasticized medical socks to send to my dad because his feet swelled up due to his illness. I mailed them off to India along with some medicine his doctor had recommended. No matter how far away I was from home, my family was never far from my mind and my heart.

On the Friday before Labor Day weekend, I wanted to head over to school early, so my brother and cousin put me on a Greyhound bus from Philadelphia to Wilkes-Barre. I got out at the public square in Wilkes-Barre and dragged my two heavy suitcases, remember, suitcases had no wheels in the early 1970s, down the three or four blocks to the school. The suitcases were filled with all the business books I'd need for class because I'd bought them with rupees in India to save money. The school was handling my room and board, and I assumed it would be open. I was wrong. Not for the first time.

My heart was pounding with excitement as I arrived at the Wilkes University campus. I was here! I got to an impressive building with the Wilkes logo on it, and, to my surprise, the door was locked. Disappointed and worried, I put my heavy bags down, hid them behind a tree, and walked around to some other buildings. Everything was locked. I didn't know it was a holiday. Nobody had told me the campus would be closed down for the Labor Day weekend!

The Susquehanna River flows right through the campus at Wilkes, and I walked to its banks and sat there on a grassy patch sobbing. Later, I lost most of my possessions when the Susquehanna flooded. I had never cried much on the hitchhiking trip, but at Wilkes University on that day, I started thinking about my dad and my mom and despairing that I didn't know what to do. I started to doubt myself and asked painful questions. Had I made a wise decision to come here? Was the admission letter from Wilkes a scam and the university out of business? What should I do now? Where would I stay? How would I get home?

Finally, I saw someone who explained the school was closed for the long weekend. I was relieved, but then I had to find a place to stay until Tuesday. Despite my somewhat muddled brain, I remembered I had walked by a YMCA on the way from the bus stop. I went there with my heavy bags, hoping for a cheap room, but this YMCA had a shelter that housed homeless senior citizens, and so for three nights, for no fee, I stayed in that shelter. The elderly residents were like no people I'd ever seen, but they undoubtedly found me strange in my Sikh turban. When I hitchhiked, I tied a bandana on my head.

Staying at the YMCA was a very humbling experience. Later in my academic life, I would walk by it many times. In fact, across the street from the 'Y' was the Westmoreland Club, an exclusive private social club where I've subsequently given speeches and welcomed dignitaries on behalf of Wilkes. But at this moment, I was profoundly homesick. I was second-guessing my decision to come to the US, worried about my father and overwhelmed by loneliness. I could see no one on campus, which was very strange coming from India, where there are hordes of people everywhere.

When the campus reopened on the day after Labor Day, I went to the office of George Ralston, the dean of students. Dean Ralston gave me unexpected bad news. The university had made a mistake, and I actually *didn't* have free room and board. Only my tuition was covered. My mind started racing. What do I do? Dean Ralston was wonderful; he was very sorry he couldn't get me into the dorms quickly, but the school had a room for the night-shift maintenance staff. I could stay there while he worked with the director of housing to get me a dorm room.

I went to the post office and wrote a letter to my parents. I didn't hide my despair, and tears dropped onto the paper, blurring my words. The letter worried my parents, which of course, wasn't my intention, but I was just a 19-year-old kid with no resources in a strange place.

I couldn't simply pick up a cell phone and call home, as there weren't any. And long-distance international calling was very costly and very difficult. You had to go to an AT&T payphone, reach an operator, and book an appointment to call. Later, whenever I did call, I came with lots of quarters, dimes, and nickels because every three minutes, the call disconnected, and you had to insert more coins. Eventually, I made a very quick call (I had to talk fast to keep down the cost) to my brother in Michigan, who was comforting. He suggested I inquire about the school's work-study program and try to get a job. It may be difficult for you to comprehend now, but the absence of cell phones and debit cards back then was extremely limiting. So was my meager budget.

Dean Ralston kept his promise, and after about four or five days of staying in that university maintenance staff room, a room was ready for me in the new men's dormitory. Things were looking up, and I continually reminded myself of the positives. Certain things have stayed with me my whole life: sitting on an airplane stewardess' jump seat, sleeping in a shelter, and George Ralston's kindness when I had no place to live. All this reinforced the life lesson I was continually learning – you can never give up. Even if obstacles block your path, you can find a way to overcome them and move forward.

It was an exciting, fascinating experience to attend college in the US, and one of the most interesting things for me was integrating into American youth culture. My roommate was a great guy from Long Island named Jerry Alexander. Jerry was a math major and a wrestler. And a big drinker. He was also a big guy with very short hair, a stark contrast to my long hair and turban. Although we were very different, we clicked and became good friends. Jerry introduced me to music like the Eagles, the Doobie Brothers, James Taylor, Santana, and all the great stuff from the early '70s.

He also introduced me to the art of brewing beer! We drank Stegmaier, a specialty Wilkes-Barre beer, which cost five cents per glass. We'd buy kegs, hang them upside down in our room, and produce even cheaper beer at three cents a glass. Jerry also introduced me to tequila and a 99-cent wine, Z Apple Wine. What a great initiation into US college life! What a great way to enjoy life on a budget! And what a great way to attract new friends because, of course, our homemade brewery was a popular attraction.

Since most of my classes were in the evening, I didn't have to wake up during the week until about 10:00 a.m. But I had come to America with the high goals of studying and succeeding, so I didn't allow partying to interfere with my studies. I bought an American car, a Pontiac LeMans, for $200. The only problem was the rust hole below the driver's feet. Every time I drove the car in the rain, water would splash on me. However, I felt blessed to own a car.

Jerry was a pretty wild guy and always had plenty of girlfriends. In October, the fraternities and sororities had dances, and Jerry invited me to double-date and go to one. It was easiest for me to meet foreign students because we shared similar experiences that comforted and linked us. The first girl I dated was a beautiful girl from Greece. The next girl I befriended was also Greek, but she was a first-generation college student. Another was a cute Slovakian from a local Wilkes-Barre coal mining family. Even my dating choices were international! Jerry gave me a new nickname, J.P., so I now had two extra identities, J.P. in the US and Sid in India.

There were maybe a dozen students in the MBA program. My very first class in an American university was managerial accounting, which was nothing like I expected. It wasn't about basic number-crunching; instead, it focused on Securities and Exchange Commission (SEC) filings, the required corporate reporting, and financial compliance. This was a foreign subject to me in a foreign country. I enjoyed the class, but a lot of it flew right over my head. Although I had a bachelor's degree in business, this subject matter was Greek to me. It was a bit of a jolt to my confidence.

The professor, Robert Capin, who later became the president of Wilkes University, was very approachable, and I sought his advice. He recommended that I go to the campus library and read the public filings of a company to understand how accounting in America works. I researched General Electric.

I read GE's complete public filings, their Form 10-Ks for the previous five years. For anyone not in the business world, a Form 10-K is an annual report filed with the Securities and Exchange Commission that describes a public company, its competition, and strategies, along with audited financial statements. The 10-K gives a complete picture of the current financials, including the income statement balance sheet and the cash flow statement, etc. This filing enables investors to gain a detailed understanding of the performance and outlook of a company they may be investing in. The form also provides management's discussion and analysis, giving a description and historical perspective on the company's financial condition. I remember Professor Capin telling me to read the footnotes, too, because that's where the company is required to explain its numbers.

Accuracy and honesty are paramount in business reporting. WorldCom and Enron weren't either of these things, and scandal and collapse followed. Chief Executive Officers (CEOs) and Chief Financial Officers (CFOs) are responsible and liable for the 10-Ks and other regulatory filings' veracity. During my past twenty-plus years as a CEO, I've been vigilant about the company's 10-Ks because I sign and certify that they are absolutely correct to my knowledge. I insist on the very highest levels of integrity and value my relationships with CFOs and Chief Accounting Officers (CAOs). CEOs must surround themselves with trusted leaders who are beyond reproach. Their educated, honest input is essential for an environment of respect, trust, and transparency in everything we do.

Professor Capin was right; reading GE's 10-Ks was the best managerial accounting and business education I could have got. It was better than the course's textbooks, and I ended up with an A in his course. To this day, partly because of that experience, I'm very quick to understand complex issues, break them down, simplify them, and formulate necessary strategies. These skills have significantly contributed to my business success, and I thank the professors at Wilkes University for allowing me to sharpen them. As you'll see, I fulfilled the promise I made many years ago on my graduate school application.

In 1972, a year after I arrived at Wilkes, I visited home. I had internships and earned some money cleaning college bathrooms, making bombs for Vietnam (I won't comment further on that), and working at Peragino's restaurant in downtown Wilkes-Barre. I also had a summer job as a waiter at Mount Airy Lodge in the Poconos. I eventually saved $10,000, but for now, I had less than $500, but it was enough to go to India. My dad was in remission, and I was confident he'd be OK. When it was time for me to leave India after visiting him, he accompanied me to the train station in the city of Lucknow, a prescient name. Except I didn't know that the image of him waving to me as I left on the train was the last time I'd ever see him. But my admiration and love for him will endure forever.

Chapter 7

THE ROAD TO BETHLEHEM AND A BANKING CAREER

A detour on the road to Bethlehem led to my banking career! No, not Bethlehem, Israel. It was an exit off the Pennsylvania Turnpike to Allentown and Bethlehem, Pennsylvania.

In the spring of 1973, toward the end of the second and final year of my MBA program, corporate recruiters visited the Wilkes University campus. Although the economy was in a recession, companies were tempting us students with promises of money, status, and opportunities for career advancement. Among the companies I interviewed with were Travelers Insurance and Sylvania Electronics, and I enthusiastically accepted a job with the latter. My first full-time job in America!

Shortly after accepting the job offer, I visited the office of Dr. Warner, dean of the department of commerce, to chat and share my news. Ultimately, the meeting would demonstrate the value of networking. Dr. Warner said that he and Dr. George Ralston, dean of students, had bumped into Wilkes' chairman of the board of trustees, Reese Jones, the CEO at First Valley Bank in Bethlehem, Pennsylvania. Mr. Jones had asked the deans to recommend a student for a job at the bank, and my name rose to the top of the list.

Dick Ehst, an executive at First Valley and a friend of Dean Ralston, had researched and recommended me to him. Dick later told me about the call he had received from Dean Ralston about a "very special aristocratic Indian" he must interview.

Dick is a brilliant guy who became a valued mentor and, later, a great friend and trusted colleague. He continued working with me when I became chairman and CEO at Sovereign Bank and Customers Bank. I explained to Dr. Warner that I'd already accepted a job at Sylvania, but Dr. Warner asked me to do him a favor anyway and see Dick and Mr. Jones at their office in Bethlehem.

I didn't pursue the matter then, but the Pennsylvania Turnpike exit beckoned. On my way to visit my brother Harry in Philadelphia in my $200 LeMans that had a rust hole under the driver's seat, I impulsively took the Allentown/ Bethlehem exit and found myself at the main offices of First Valley Bank at 535 Main Street. I became a bit flustered because I couldn't remember the name of the bank president Dr. Warner and Dean Ralston wanted me to see. Undeterred, I nonchalantly asked a secretary. Also, I didn't have an appointment with Mr. Jones. On top of that, I was wearing jeans, a t-shirt, and long hair, the typically scruffy uniform for university students in the 60s and 70s. My appearance certainly wasn't appropriate for a business interview. Nevertheless, Mr. Jones' assistant ushered me into his office. She later told me she had thought I was a friend of Reese Jones' son, which was a lucky mistake for me.

Mr. Jones and I exchanged pleasantries, and he asked about my background. As usual, I had plenty to say and animatedly described my upbringing, hitchhiking adventures, and classes. The conversation shifted to the topic of banking. Mr. Jones began discussing the restrictive nature of banking at the time. He explained that you had to stay in your local county, or the directly neighboring counties, to open new branches. I wasn't sure where the conversation was heading, but Mr. Jones continued. He asked the question that led to my job offer, "How do you think the bank can overcome this geographical obstacle and open more successful branches?" I suggested we analyze the successful existing branches to figure out what three or four things make them work well. Then, I continued, we consider a similar model whenever we look at a potential new location.

I got a 4.0 GPA at Wilkes, and I aced this interview too. Mr. Jones hired me on the spot. However, I thanked him for the kind offer and told him I'd already accepted a job at Sylvania. Now it was his turn not to be deterred. He said, "Look, you haven't started there yet. Whatever Sylvania is paying, I'll pay you $500 more."

Five hundred dollars! I planned to return to India once I'd made $10,000, and now, I already had five percent of my goal. My starting salary was $8,500. Eight years later, I was earning six figures. I didn't need any further incentive and immediately accepted Mr. Jones' offer.

This moment was my introduction to the banking industry, where I've spent my entire career to this day. Later, I learned it was Dick Ehst's recommendation to Reese that had sealed the deal to hire me. I owe Dick a lot for getting me into the banking business.

Along with my MBA education at Wilkes and continuing education experiences at Harvard, Dartmouth, and elsewhere, which I'll describe later, Reese Jones and First Valley schooled me well. They provided my formative, hands-on education in the banking industry. And perhaps, most significantly, the people I worked with there made an enduring impact on me both personally and professionally. I've never, ever looked back at the "road not taken," that is, the Pennsylvania Turnpike straight to my brother's temporary home in Philadelphia.

Now, here I was in Bethlehem, Pennsylvania, renting an apartment on the south side of town with a roommate, Brent, a student at Lehigh University. My rent was only $250 a month, and I enjoyed the benefit of a de facto house mother, a sweet, older woman, Esther, who lived alone above us and who cooked us meals and checked on us.

I didn't mind living frugally. It was a tradeoff I was more than willing to make to achieve my goal. Remember, I had hitchhiked with no money, and now, I intended to save $10,000 to return to India. I did try to supplement my income during my first two weeks at First Valley Bank by taking a part-time job selling vacuum cleaners. That didn't last. I needed to focus all my efforts on my full-time job. Besides, banking was much more exciting than household cleaning products.

Reese Jones, my boss at First Valley Bank, became my valued mentor, and I remain grateful for his tutelage. I always called him Mr. Jones but will refer to him as Reese here. Reese disproved the prevailing notion in the 1970s that bankers' hours were cushy, i.e., beginning at 9:00 a.m. and on the golf course by 3:00 p.m. Nothing could be further from the truth for Reese; he was hardworking, energetic, and driven.

Reese was a true visionary, full of passion and innovative ideas about growing the bank. He was trained as an economist and became a self-made chairman of the board and CEO with an impressive resume. In addition to attending Wilkes, Reese earned a master's degree in economics from the University of Pennsylvania's Wharton School.

He envisioned the future of banking, statewide banking, by literally pushing boundaries. To realize his vision, he attracted a team of people he could trust and inspired them. Reese was young, in his late 30s or early 40s, and hand-picked an inner circle of like-minded young people. I was honored to become part of that circle of senior executives, comprising Dick Ehst, Tim Widener, Reese, and me. The relationships I built at First Valley have had an enduring impact on me. Dick Ehst particularly has been a lifelong mentor, colleague, and great friend.

Reese assigned me to another young guy, Mac Walker, in the corporate planning department as a management trainee. Mac was notably absent from Reese's inner circle. He was a typical blue-blood type of banker from a well-to-do family that owned car dealerships. I ultimately replaced Mac, whose style was unsuited to Reese's creative thinking and quick temperament. Mac was highly analytical, but he didn't communicate well with senior management. I liked Mac, appreciated his insights, and learned from his strengths and shortcomings. However, my primary lesson was the importance of communicating, not just reporting, and pivoting when necessary. In sharp contrast to Mac, Reese could adapt to change and make change happen. His vision extended to recognizing my potential and that of others in his inner circle.

At the age of twenty-three, I was vice president of corporate planning at First Valley Bank.

Reese held weekly senior management meetings and appointed me as the group's secretary. Those meetings provided me with unparalleled on-the-job corporate training. I studiously took notes and minutes and followed up with

Reese, detailing what had transpired, asking questions, and even making suggestions. I was thrilled by this opportunity.

One of my corporate planning responsibilities was applying regression analyses to identify the historical results of our banks. Then, based on the way they performed, I projected the expectations. It was simple statistics. I prepared a book on every single branch we had, including the history of the branch, where they were heading, how they were performing, and how that performance compared with other branches. Then I would take the data and, using a punch-card system, represent it visually. What are the four or five things that make for a successful branch? Is it population? Income? Traffic? Do storefront banks do better than freestanding ones?

At that time, First Valley had about twelve or fifteen branches and was called a "contiguous county bank." We were in Northampton County and Pennsylvania, and you could only add a branch to counties that touched your county. Reese's vision transcended these limited boundaries. His innovation was to *buy* little banks in addition to opening up branches.

Reese expected and received extreme loyalty from many of the people who worked for him. And it was earned. He created a solid corporate culture that rewarded hard work and inventive thinking. Reese modeled how business leaders act effectively. Nevertheless, like any leader, his style and way of thinking were a mixed bag. Yes, he had a vision and passion for the future of banking. However, along with that level of energy and focus came impatience and intolerance for negative comments, no matter how on-point they may be. Open-mindedness is essential, so vision isn't necessarily enough, especially in publicly traded companies.

The lending side of First Valley was somewhat flawed. Since Reese hadn't assigned a strong chief lending officer, he basically made all the decisions himself about who should get the loans. And the most important critical success factor in banking is when you make a loan, you must have a very, very strong plan for getting the money back. Further, *identifying* critical success factors for any decision is absolutely essential.

Along with Dick Ehst and me, there was another key executive, Tim

Widener. Tim was in charge of operations, and Dick was in charge of the rest of the bank. As for me, I did whatever was needed. I relished the opportunity and once told Reese he could give me any challenge, and if it was humanly possible, I'd do it. He took me at my word. One day he and Dick called upon me to clean up and run what they called the "mess" of the mortgage department. I hardly knew anything about mortgages, but if Reese wanted me to run the department, I'd figure it out. I loved that assignment; not only did we fix the mess, but I also learned a lot about leadership.

Dick Ehst became a great friend of mine and still is. He's just four years older than me, six foot one, a former marine, and the smartest guy I know. He's a genuine, authentic leader. When you need somebody on your side who will never abandon you, that's Dick. He and I clicked from day one. Dick's dad was also a very special man, and he and I became good friends as well. He had been a military commander like my dad and served as a fighter pilot in the Air Force during the Korean and Vietnam wars.

One of Dick's responsibilities was operating efficiency. A brilliant idea that Dick, Reese, and Tim conceived for the bank involved clearing checks. Remember, there was no electronic banking at this time. The Federal Reserve ran everything, so checks traveled by land and would take at least three to five days to clear. That time lag was problematic.

How did we solve this problem? Our company bought a small plane!

We brainstormed using a plane to minimize our check-clearance time. It was easy to implement our vision because we convinced Dick's father to fly the plane, which he did for very little money. Now our customers could have access to their deposits the next morning. Thus, we could offer our customers next-day credit. This innovation presaged the immediacy of electronic banking.

Reese was always attracted to people who found solutions. When Tim and Dick came up with this plane flight next-day-clearance idea, and Dick said his dad could do it, Reese loved it. It had a huge impact not only on our operations but also on our image. We were burnishing our reputation as visionaries who got things done. A little bank in Bethlehem with its own plane.

We'd go from our office to pick up the checks in Bethlehem at about 5:00 p.m. Then, Dick's dad would make the twenty-five-minute flight to Wilkes-Barre, where we had a branch office. From Wilkes Barre, we'd fly to Philadelphia and get the checks to the Federal Reserve Bank for clearing before the cutoff time. We made speed a huge advantage of banking with us. The plane also provided a great personal advantage to me because I'd sometimes jump in with Dick's father and fly from Bethlehem to Philadelphia. This way, I could visit friends, and what a thrill it was for me to see the lights and towers from the skies of Philadelphia. The experience later inspired me to become a student pilot myself.

Reese not only changed the way people banked, but he also changed the community of Bethlehem. He inspired us to plan and execute a concept for a shopping area and a new bank building. He built One Bethlehem Plaza as our headquarters, then the tallest building in Bethlehem. With Dick in charge, the project was completed on time and on budget, which was a rare construction feat. Reese was the first to attach an indoor mall in the downtown area, putting money into real community revitalization in the 1970s. Further, he made our headquarters a public attraction by putting in a skating rink, which could also be used for events in the summer. The complex became Bethlehem's mini-Rockefeller Center, and Dick had another brilliant idea to start a music festival there. It's still going today and has become one of Bethlehem's greatest downtown attractions; MusikFest.

At the time, I was still living frugally. I saved $500 from my monthly paychecks and continued living with Brent. I could have afforded a nicer place, but I was committed to accumulating $10,000 to return to India. I also kept my cheap little car, which was fine with me. It was a big deal when later, I bought an orange Volkswagen Beetle with a sunroof. After a while, I got raises, and when we built the new building, Reese gave me an office. I took over as head of corporate planning from Mac Walker, who had left the bank.

I finally got my green card and became a permanent resident of the United States. It was time to celebrate, but there were about to be more unexpected detours and decisions ahead.

While I was at a business conference in Chicago, my brother Harry called with devastating news. I remember his exact words, "Dad's no more." My father had succumbed to cancer. I thought about the train station in Lucknow and the time my dad waved to me as I was hanging out of the train window. It was the last time I saw him, between my first and second year at Wilkes University. So many of his lessons now meant even more to me than ever before. Foremost in my memory was his exhortation to know your mission in life and stick to it.

I immediately took a flight from Chicago to Roanoke, Virginia, to meet Harry. I intended to move back to India, but Harry insisted I stay in the US. As the eldest son, he would go to India and take care of what needed to be done with our family. Harry was making good money and was quite capable. He assured me that I was honoring our father's memory by working and making something of myself in America. So, sadly, I returned to Bethlehem from Roanoke.

In India, my mom was a wreck, and Harry brought her and my sister back to live with him outside Roanoke in a town called Pearisburg, Virginia. Harry had just gotten married to Suzanne, who's now my sister-in-law. She's a lovely person, born and raised in Texas, but it was very difficult for my mom. She was seventeen when she and my father met in 1947, and they endured that dangerous trip together on the train from India to Pakistan. As strong a woman as she was, she had depended on my dad to make decisions. Fortunately, my brother and sister-in-law helped my mom raise our younger sister Hareeta, and I found it reassuring that I lived in Bethlehem, just an eight-hour drive away.

Not long after that, in 1976, Reese Jones went on vacation to Florida with some friends and one of our board members. While on a boat, he had a heart attack and died. He was still very young, in his mid-forties. Now my dad was gone after a long illness, and my mentor was dead very unexpectedly. It was a painful double whammy.

With Reese gone, suddenly, there was a power vacuum at First Valley.

Dick Ehst was the logical internal candidate to be moved up, but he was perceived as having been too closely aligned with Reese. Instead, the First Valley board of directors filled the CEO position with another professional banker named John Howell, who had been in charge of corporate banking at Girard Bank, a large established bank in Philadelphia.

When John Howell came in, within the first ten days, he distanced himself from Dick. He brought a new team with him from his bank in Philadelphia, which is natural in the course of business. The upheaval continued, and Dick Ehst and Tim Widener became frustrated and decided to leave First Valley in 1978. I was devastated and expressed my feelings to John, fully expecting to be let go any day. But for the time being, I kept working for John in corporate planning and marketing, the same job I had under Reese and Dick. I needed to make money to fulfill my goals.

Not long after John started, I received a brochure in the mail about an executive marketing and strategic planning program at Harvard Business School. I had *always* wanted to go to Harvard, it represented the pinnacle of educational achievement, and I was always eager to learn more. I told John that I very much wanted to attend the program. He categorically refused. John's attitude stood in sharp contrast to Reese's values. Reese approved whatever you wanted that would benefit the corporation or your performance. He trusted his employees enough to allow them room for growth. I went back to John one more time and told him that if the barrier to my attending Harvard were the cost, I'd pay for it myself. He again refused, and I knew that to grow, it was time for me to find another job.

Coincidentally, around this time, Bob Swanick, whom I had brought to First Valley to do some management training and development, called me. Bob's consulting firm, Fairmont Training, worked with a big New Jersey bank called American National Bank. It eventually became Horizon Bank, and then, after that, Chemical Bank/Chase. Bob offered to reach out to an executive vice president there on my behalf. I wasted no time and made an appointment to see his contact, Phil Hudson.

With youthful enthusiasm, I drove to Morristown, New Jersey, in my new orange Volkswagen Beetle to meet Phil. And I got hired again after one interview.

I became American National Bank's director of marketing. And the Harvard program I had been hoping to attend? When I mentioned it to Phil, not only did he tell me I could attend, but he also told me the bank would pay for the program. What a completely different attitude from John at First Valley. This confirmed the wisdom of my decision to work for Phil at American National. It also reinforced the value of risk-taking.

Phil was active in the top tier of bank marketing associations, and he was the head of the Retail Banking Association at that time. He was well-known in the industry; of course, I'd heard of him. I'd also known of Jeff Lord, the CEO at American National, who came from Citibank and Manufacturers Hanover in New York. I was excited about the challenges ahead and confident that my new position would open more doors for me. Because now, instead of being in a contiguous county bank in Pennsylvania, I would be getting into the New York, New Jersey, and international banking scenes.

With Phil's offer to work at American National in hand, I walked into John Howell's office at First Valley and politely told him I was leaving. He tried to dissuade me in a private meeting in the executive suite of our boardroom on the eleventh floor of One Bethlehem Plaza. Over sandwiches, John made excuses for not being able to retain Dick and Tim and said he was willing to send me to Harvard. He told me how much he valued and respected me and how he really didn't want to lose me. But somehow, I didn't think he was being 100 percent authentic. I certainly didn't have a warm feeling about him as I'd had with Reese and Dick, or with Phil Hudson at American National, for that matter.

I told John that I had given my word and intended to follow through on it. I didn't second-guess myself, but this situation wasn't easy. It was a considerable risk to change jobs, and I'd never done it before, but I'd always had a spirit of adventure, and it extended to taking the risk of accepting the new job at American National Bank.

Although I appreciated John's belated effort to keep me at First Valley, I didn't appreciate his efforts to change the bank. He would routinely cut costs at the expense of quality and success. Instead of a leader, the company now had a bureaucrat in charge. John got rid of the plane we used to make same-day deposits available. He got rid of a lot of good people, and he got rid of much of the culture, processes, and progress that had made First Valley successful. We had some loan problems, but none that couldn't be fixed. Under John, First Valley went back to being just an average bank.

I felt grateful for the opportunities I had at First Valley and proud of what I had accomplished. It was my first job straight out of college, and I had risen to be one of the bank's senior executives. As I've said, it was like getting paid for an education in banking, management, and leadership. I still wanted to go to Harvard, and I eventually did. I also felt very good about how our team there had worked together towards common goals. But the place soured for me, and many others, after Reese died. We were all used to accomplishments being rewarded rather than bureaucracy taking center stage.

Banking is an industry built on relationships, and Phil Hudson and I connected personally. Even during my initial interview, Phil asked about my hobbies instead of just quizzing me on my career in banking. His eyes lit up when I told him I'd like to get a pilot's license. He shared an enthusiasm for flying and went way beyond me; he eventually got his instrument pilot's license, whereas I only got my student pilot's license. In fairness, I didn't pursue flying after fracturing my hip.

Phil Hudson had an entrepreneurial style and, like Reese, a sense of how to be ahead of the curve. Phil demonstrated leadership traits that I have tried to emulate. He encouraged me and everyone on his team to succeed and, in so doing, to make American National Bank a success.

After I joined Phil, American National was among the first banks in the nation to offer home equity loans. Additionally, we made it one of the first banks in the US to promote Visa cards and ATMs. They had existed in some form, but we figured out how to market them. We were also among the first banks in the nation to introduce sales and service recognition and rewards programs for our team members, making them like an Academy Awards ceremony. It wasn't only simple and unique; it was *innovative*.

Now that I was at American National, I was looking forward to heading to Cambridge, Massachusetts, for the Harvard Business School's marketing and strategic planning program. I couldn't wait. This was the Harvard Business School (HBS) program for mid-management executives looking to add to their knowledge of marketing and strategy. It's a highly competitive and selective program with three to five times as many applicants as are admitted. Further, it cost over $5,000 to attend, so you better believe that all the participants were highly motivated.

Arriving at Harvard for this three-day program was an emotional and humbling achievement for me. I think I still have the key to the room I stayed in; it symbolizes the many doors I've opened. It's hard to describe the moment when something you have always longed for finally arrives. I'm fortunate to have had this experience several times, including long ago when I arrived in London as a kid.

My participation in the HBS marketing and strategic planning program was an outgrowth of my continued drive for professional development. It also confirmed my certainty that Harvard's business curriculum had tremendous theoretical and practical value. When I became a CEO, I enrolled in its specialized "Leadership for Presidents and CEOs" program. This was an annual, week-long intensive learning experience.

One of the special features of HBS is the way learning is structured. We formed a cohort of eight people, and each participant was a chief executive in their respective businesses. I've met people from all different industries, continents, and economies. I've participated in the CEO program fourteen times, and, except for a few sessions, I've been the only banker.

Harvard is known for its case study methodology, and we each used our own experiences to analyze real-life cases. In so doing, we became like each other's personal board of directors, openly sharing our ideas. You had to stay on your toes because the professor would call on you anytime during the case study sessions. Of course, there was much more than academics to the Harvard experience.

There were also phenomenal opportunities to network with highly talented individuals. We would meet up with groups of MBA students and have drinks and dinner together every Thursday, which was a marvelous two-way learning experience. As with the Young Presidents' Organization forums, where members have achieved significant leadership roles at a young age, the HBS program connected me with "the best and the brightest."

If you attend at least ten leadership programs, you are considered the equivalent of a Harvard Business School MBA (with Harvard alumni status). However, my motivation was to learn from the best international business minds, *not* gain a fancy credential. Subsequent sessions were invitation only, so it was crucial to do well to be invited back. It was an honor for me to participate in 14 one-week sessions. In addition to studying on the Harvard campus in Cambridge, I attended sessions in Shanghai and Mumbai, which furthered my engagement with current international business thinking.

Attending the executive leadership program at Harvard Business School was a continuation of my life-long quest for self-improvement, and it helped prepare me for some of my most consequential decisions yet to come.

With my dad, the last time I saw him.

With my son Sam, when he was in high school at an Eagles football game.

With my son Sam and daughter Luvleen after NYSE bell ringing ceremony. All of us at one time were CEO's of NYSE listed companies.

A relaxing moment with my granddaughters.

At old course, St. Andrews, Scotland.

At my favorite golf club LedgeRock after a good round.

With Sherry in Kashmir, India.

A happy moment with Sherry.

Father and son golfing trip to Orlando

With my Forum buddies in Bahamas.

Our family picture at Times Square when CUBI first listed on NASDAQ.

Golf outing to California with Dave, Sarb, and Harry (my brother).

With our son Samvir when he was 5 months old.

At Pahalgam, Kashmir, shortly after we got married.

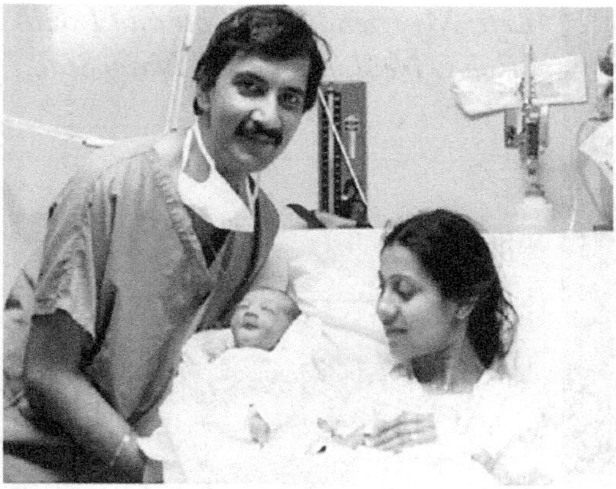

Birth of our son Samvir.

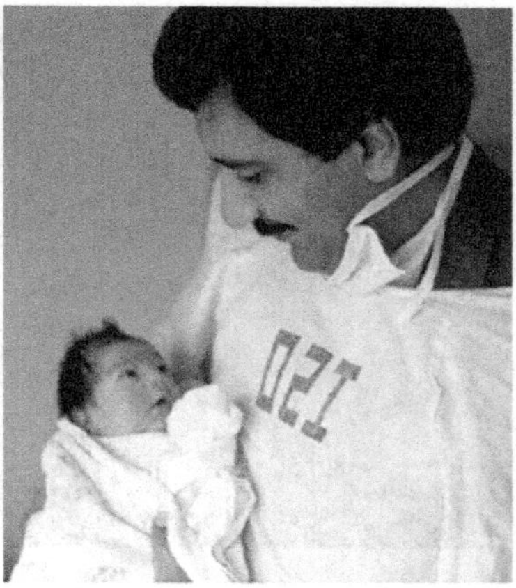

With my daughter Luvleen when she was two days old.

Left: At Masai Mara in Kenya with our children.

With our grandson Lian less than a day old.

Left: Sherry and I at a friend's daughter's wedding

Left: My friend Dick Ehst and I with Rob O'Neill, former US Navy Seal.

Story in N.J. Star Ledge on Mother's Day about Mom and I

My sister, brother, and I with mom.

Right; family portrait of my parents when I was 1 year old.

Sherry and I with British P.M. Margaret Thatcher

Sherry with President Bill Clinton.

Having dinner with President George Bush.

WIth His Holiness the 14th Dalai Lama.

Chapter 8

BANKING ON MY FUTURE

Career-changing meetings can happen in likely places like a classroom at Harvard Business School or unexpected places like a hotel bar in Hanover, New Hampshire, or a basement restaurant in Ephrata, Pennsylvania.

As I've discussed, when I worked at American National Bank, my mentor Phil Hudson heartily approved of continuing professional education. He enabled me to attend the Harvard Business School marketing and strategic planning program for management executives, for which I'm very grateful. I was also fortunate to attend the Tuck School of Business at Dartmouth's leadership and strategic impact program for high-potential executives. There, I met an individual who opened doors to two more banks for me.

Paul Wieand was also attending the Dartmouth program, and we met at the hotel bar while at the conference. At the time, Paul was the president and CEO of Independence Bancorp, so clearly, we shared many common interests. We made small talk at first and then began discussing strategies and ideas. Our conversation became a friendly debate about how to succeed in banking and business. My position was that it's all about people; Paul's was that it's all about numbers. We stayed in touch and subsequently revisited this conversation several times.

Paul also knew some of my former colleagues at First Valley. Later, I learned that he had asked Dick to recommend a great retail banker. Fortunately, Dick named me, and Paul ended up recruiting me to leave American National Bank to work at Independence Bank Corp. and its lead bank, Bucks County Bank, where he was CEO. The bank experienced rapid growth during the five years I was there, garnering widespread recognition, and I rose to become the Chief Operating Officer (COO) and divisional coordinator. I was having a lot of fun doing what I love, helping both the bank and the customers succeed. But there were rocky times ahead for the bank.

Paul and I had complementary skills that enabled us to tackle the challenges facing Independence and, later, Penn Savings. He was highly intelligent and approached problem-solving with financial research. In contrast, my approach was to emphasize the people side and the customers, not just the numbers. To me, superlative execution depends on people, and in banking, the most important criterion for giving a loan is the customers' ability to repay it. Most of the time, Paul worked in his office studying. But I spent most of *my* time interacting with people rather than sitting behind a desk. Our primary difference can be summed up as Paul had a high IQ (intelligence), and I had a good EQ (emotional intelligence).

Independence's board became dissatisfied with Paul because they wanted a more execution-oriented strategist, and, unfortunately, he was asked to leave due to differences between him and our chairman at the time. Paul's downfall was caused by the same fundamental issue that had plagued Mac Walker at First Valley; they both put too much emphasis on theoretical analysis and not enough on communication, marketing, and interpersonal relationships. Paul enlisted my help to save his position, and I tried my best, but in the end, it was a board decision, not mine as management.

Gradually, I became discontented at Independence Bank. Too much time was spent in discussion and not enough in action. I'm a forward-thinker and change-maker, and the bank's stagnation was anathema to me. Additionally, I thrive on deal-making. I worried that the tide had changed at the bank, and they were heading toward unpreventable failure. I began looking around, and a new opportunity arose.

In 1986, Paul was offered a job at Penn Savings Bank, and he recruited me by predicating his acceptance on bringing me along as COO. Paul uttered one word that enticed me: equity. I agreed to enter discussions with Penn, a savings and loan (S&L) based in Wyomissing, Pennsylvania.

Paul had also enlisted Dick, my dear friend and former colleague, to persuade me to consider the job at Penn seriously. Dick was president of a troubled private bank at that time. Recently, Dick reminded me of one of my initial hesitations. Penn was in the heart of Southeastern Pennsylvania, which has a concentrated community of Pennsylvania Dutch. My concern was that a young Indian fellow like me wouldn't be readily accepted there. Nevertheless, Dick's unwavering encouragement and the word "equity" echoed in my ears, and I was open to conversations.

I attended a meeting to discuss the position with some members of the board of Penn Savings in a dark, rather dingy basement restaurant in Ephrata, near Reading. The environment somewhat surprised me. I had become used to bank operations being conducted in boardrooms with polished mahogany conference tables, beautiful skylights, and attached kitchens. As I later discovered, Penn Savings didn't even have space for offices for Paul and me at their headquarters initially. Spoiler alert: from these humble beginnings, the bank became the 17th largest bank in the US and a Fortune 500 company during my tenure.

The group interview was one of the easiest I'd ever participated in. Penn Savings was a troubled institution, and when I was asked what I'd do to turn it around, I didn't hesitate. My previous banking experience prepared me to prioritize what can be done to create value. Value for customers, value for investors, and value for team members.

It appeared that Penn Savings and I would be a good match, but, as with any major life change, I needed to consider the pros and cons carefully.

❁❁❁

So many decisions came so quickly during those busy years in the early to mid-1980s. The best decision I ever made was to marry Sherry, whom I had known since childhood. Our families were friends, but she and I had lost contact over the years. On one of my trips back to India, our uncles proposed that we meet again and perhaps get married. It's common for Indian marriages to be arranged this way.

Sherry and I wed in 1978 and bought a home in Bucks County. However, it was a difficult adjustment for Sherry to leave her family in India for the utter foreignness of the US. She was only twenty years old, and we hadn't intimately known each other for long. It also didn't help that long-distance calling was difficult and expensive in those days before FaceTime and similar apps.

Sherry gradually adapted, and the birth of our children filled both of our lives with joy. Sammy (now known as Sam) was born in 1983, and there are no words to describe the extraordinary experience of holding him for the first time. Three years later, in 1986, my daughter Luvleen was born, bringing the same feelings of overwhelming joy.

Today, as adults, Sam and Luvleen continue to give Sherry and me great joy. I'm proud not only of their accomplishments but also of the human beings they've become. Both have exhibited the utmost integrity in their personal and professional lives. I credit Sherry for much of their success; she gave up her career as a management trainee at Prudential to be a full-time mother while I was often away, working at a breakneck pace and traveling on business.

Neither of us could have imagined that one day, Sam, Luvleen, and I would achieve a historic feat; a son, daughter, and father would all serve as CEOs of NYSE publicly traded companies at the same time.

❁❁❁

In many ways, my vision of my family life and career was taking shape barely a decade after I arrived in the US.

I accepted the offer from Penn Savings because the challenge was appealing. Even more importantly, so was the compensation package. My current arrangement had only been salary plus bonuses. Penn offered me about a five to ten percent equity position in the form of stock appreciation rights and stock options. These returns depended on a prosperous initial public offering (IPO) to take the bank public and the bank being successfully built. Accepting the job was a high-risk, high-reward decision. Turns out, it was a high-reward bonanza for me.

Imagine my surprise at an initial board meeting when I learned that the bank's priorities focused on minutiae, like the color of the logo and the size of the boardroom. A failing bank more concerned with interior decor than with strategic planning and execution? My work was cut out for me, and I jumped in!

Let me contextualize Penn Savings Bank's problems by describing the prevailing financial environment. It was bleak. There was a high failure rate in the banking industry during the protracted S&L crisis, which extended from 1980 to 1989. When President Ronald Reagan took office in 1981, the US was experiencing its worst economic recession since the Great Depression.

The first S&L (also known as thrift) was established in Pennsylvania in 1831 to enable Americans to pursue their dream of home ownership. Therefore, their primary function was to provide residential long-term, fixed-rate mortgages. The banks' funds relied on deposits with a relatively short maturity period, making them vulnerable to interest rate increases. Coupled with high inflation, interest rates steadily increased between 1980 and 1989.

When interest rates rise, mortgage values go down. Variable-rate mortgages were not yet widely available. The federal government's deregulation of S&Ls didn't help either. To make matters even messier, Penn Savings, like other S&Ls, responded by getting involved too quickly in too many risky, out-of-state loans that, although on variable rates, were doomed to default. The result was sustained significant losses.

When Paul and I came on board, the numbers told a grim story. Penn Savings had been formed following a merger between two Pennsylvania-based S&Ls, one in Wyomissing and one in Lancaster. It was a bank with $400 million in assets, with twelve percent nonperforming loans and only three percent capital. That was bad news. That meant *negative* capital. Clearly, the number one priority was to get capital coming in. The million-dollar question was, "How?"

Once again, Paul's and my complementary skillsets made us a good team to turn Penn Savings around. I continued cultivating my interpersonal skills and self-awareness at a leadership workshop that Phil Hudson had sent me to, the Experience Compression Lab (ECL). I underwent various psychological assessments and participated in role-playing scenarios. Listening attentively and internalizing others' feedback is a key component of ECL's training.

Similarly, I was positively impacted by my monthly participation in the Young Presidents Organization (YPO) forums. Its central tenet is that leadership development accelerates with networking. Accordingly, it opened me to the concept of having a "personal board of directors" through the forums, reliable businesspeople who turn into valuable advisors and trusted friends. I also benefited from training at Dale Carnegie classes, which stress understanding your strengths and weaknesses and interpersonal relationships.

I continually aspire to be a reflective businessperson who can evaluate myself and situations and motivate others in the pursuit of improvement. And my immediate pursuit now was to save Penn Savings from the brink of financial disaster. To succeed, it was necessary to identify the problems and what caused them and then go a step further and learn from them.

Paul and I developed a four-pronged strategic focus, essentially, critical success factors, to rescue the bank: (1) high asset quality, (2) low-interest rate risk, (3) low-efficiency ratios, and (4) service excellence with an emphasis on team members. Yes, we needed to increase revenues twice as fast as expenses and effectively manage risks. But we also needed to invest in people to create a leadership culture of continuous improvement. Further, we needed to be committed to ensuring our customers' satisfaction and success. When asked about their experiences with the bank, customers should say, "Wow!"

The corollary of all these success factors is the basic one I've already mentioned, i.e., high asset quality by fixing the existing loan problems and ensuring that customers can repay their loans. So, I insisted on systematically evaluating the cash flow and character of all our borrowers as the principal means to recoup our investments to build a strong credit culture. It's straight-forward. Consider the borrowers' characters and whether there's sufficient collateral and, if not, secure other assets to use as personal guarantees. It comes down to experienced relationship bankers making informed decisions.

Penn had violated almost all these basic principles and gotten into a mess. There were inflated appraisals and no cash flow analyses. Further, there was no contingency planning. The bank did not know the borrowers or the neighborhoods they were buying into. The managers and executives had never seen or educated themselves about where their money was going. They just wanted to make variable-rate loans as interest rates were rising, and by focusing only on the interest rates, they neglected the most significant critical success factor, *credit risk*, resulting in superior asset quality.

Paul researched the models of banks that had successfully been saved from failure. Two, in particular, stood out. Allied Bank Corp. in Texas and Bank One in Ohio. I owe a debt to Paul for educating me on the topic; we used these models as the bases for our strategies at Penn. Further, Paul and I both believed that a banking institution should be built the way America was built. That meant having a centralized federal group that sets overall policy *and* separate decentralized entities responsible for execution under the federal umbrella.

Not only should there be a federal "constitution" outlining the basic principles (responsibilities, rights, and requirements), but there should also be individual state ones defining how financial institutions can operate autonomously while adhering to federal regulations and risk management principles.

Paul and I agreed that the name "Penn Savings Bank" did not effectively articulate our vision, and we decided to change it. As we brainstormed, we thought of the words "federal" and "independence," but they were already too widely used. In fact, we had just come from Independence Bancorp. So what did we do? We used a thesaurus! Aha! "Sovereign" perfectly expressed our intent.

That's how Sovereign Bank was born in 1988.

Along with the new name, we designed a new logo. The inspiration came to me as I was leaving my house one day. There was a street lantern in front of my home. Aha! A lantern illustrated our home mortgage business. Then I asked myself what made Burger King and McDonald's logos stand out. They were red and white. And that was that. Sovereign Bank's identity was manifested. We didn't use any expensive marketing consultants to come up with our name and logo. We used common sense.

Shortly thereafter, we established Sovereign Bancorp. There are many advantages to raising capital if you form a holding company. Five months after I came on board, we had cleaned up a good portion of the bank's loan portfolio sufficiently to go public and successfully secured $12 million in the IPO. The bank was healthier, and the promise that I'd receive stock ultimately materialized. When I left Sovereign, the company's value was $12 billion.

Unfortunately, Paul again alienated some important members of Sovereign's board of directors. There was a mutual parting of ways in 1989. Paul had wanted to sell and cash out, whereas the board and I believed opportunity lies in times of financial crisis. One of the directors, Dan Rothermel, with whom I developed a wonderful relationship we maintain to this day, clearly remembers the decisive meeting about Paul's dismissal. Dan tells how the board met privately on a Saturday morning. Of course, the question of who should take over from Paul arose. My name came up, and the board heartily endorsed me as the best candidate. Dan knew where I lived, coincidentally about a mile-and-a-half away from the meeting location, and he was asked to drive to my home to see if I would join them. Remember, without cell phones we relied on face-to-face communication.

At the age of 38, in 1989, I became CEO and president of both Sovereign Bancorp and Sovereign Bank. In roughly four hundred days, we did it. We turned Sovereign into a well-capitalized, billion-dollar-plus bank.

Among my other strategic initiatives was embarking on opening new branches and making new acquisitions to build revenues that were twice our overhead expenses. We identified problem banks to buy cheap and turn around. Unlike the days before statewide and interstate banking, we were no longer limited to contiguous counties. So, New England, the mid-Atlantic states, and elsewhere were fair game.

Our first major acquisition was a small institution in Bucks County, Pennsylvania, called Yardley Savings and Loan. Like every new company Sovereign acquired after that, whenever appropriate, the acquisition would preserve its management and place in the community. Having rid ourselves of our bad loans, the bank's expansion was gaining forward momentum. This was remarkable. While the US was experiencing the S&L crisis, we were strong and opportunistic. While other S&Ls were struggling and failing, we were building a highly successful bank.

I endeavored to create a corporate culture of not only institutional improvement but also personal growth. I was so committed to the principles I learned in my professional development seminars that I made attendance at a Dale Carnegie course a requirement for everyone in a leadership role. Additionally, I held leadership to a high standard of operational excellence and integrity.

After six months of working at Sovereign at a frenetic pace, I recognized that I badly needed a break. Sadly, I got a break I didn't need; a fractured hip. My brother-in-law had invited me to go skiing later in the year in Zermatt, Switzerland. Before going to the Alps, I thought skiing in Pennsylvania a few times would be good preparation and a much-needed diversion. I went skiing with a friend on Doe Mountain in Allentown, Pennsylvania, one evening after work. When I informed my assistant Ruth Wikes of my plans, her parting words were, "don't come back on crutches." But I did. With screws in my hip and crutches under my arms, I still had to fight for the bank by going on road shows to raise capital from investment bankers and high-net-worth individuals as part of the IPO process.

One of our investors was an astute man named Fred Jaindl, who had become a 19.9 percent shareholder in 1988. Fred was appointed chairman of Sovereign Bancorp, our holding company. After Paul's departure from the company in 1989, I remained the CEO and president. Fred was a hugely successful landowner and turkey farmer whose turkeys were often the ones pardoned at the White House Thanksgiving ceremony. Although Fred liked to micromanage, we got along fine. He was pleased that whenever he called, whether at 7:00 a.m. or 9:00 p.m., I was there working. By 1995, Fred had seen his role and investment grow from a few million dollars to over $20 million.

With big money often comes big drama. At a board meeting sometime in 1995, Fred suddenly banged the gavel and made a motion to appoint so and so to the board. His objective was to gain control, sell the business and, thus, monetize his investment. Fred had already spoken to four of the eight board members ahead of time to secure their approval and assumed that the others would follow along. When I spoke up at the meeting and asked Fred what he was doing, he brusquely quieted me. In response, I made a passionate speech about our company's values, saying they were based on mutual trust and respect. I implored further that the maneuverings in the boardroom were contrary to our core principles and common objectives.

I continued, saying that if we wanted to add a couple of new directors to the board, we should discuss it but don't go about it by staging a coup to take over. Four members voiced their agreement with me. We were at a four-to-four stalemate. This angered Fred, and he walked out, saying he'd do whatever he could to prevail. Later, I tried to appease Fred privately and asked him to explain what he wanted to achieve, discuss it openly, and reconvene the board. He flat-out refused.

I then called my outside counsel, Joe Harenza, at Stephens & Lee, a local law firm at the time, to explore an appropriate course of action. In his opinion, Fred was violating a slew of banking laws, corporate governance policies and procedures, and SEC rules, all of which require a shareholder to put forth their intentions publicly and not forcibly seize control. Joe advised me that to really get Fred's attention and prevent disaster, I needed to engage the top New York law firm, Skadden Arps.

With no hope of a conciliatory meeting, I was advised that my only recourse was to do something very unusual for a CEO of a publicly traded company, namely, file suit against the chairman of the board. I tried pleading with Fred again and had breakfast with him and his board friends, but they were united and intractable. After consulting with the four other board members who supported my position, including Dan Rothermel, I took action as I was driving down the Pennsylvania Turnpike.

I authorized a complaint to be filed against our chairman of the board.

It was a costly battle. Fred hired Rodge Cohen, a high-powered attorney from Sullivan & Cromwell, also a New York powerhouse firm. And when I called another board meeting, Fred showed up with Rodge, who wasn't allowed in because he was neither a director nor a company lawyer. After

Rodge left, Fred finally proposed a resolution that involved both sides choosing directors and appointing an independent one. The proposal was conditioned on our paying all of Fred's legal expenses, totaling over $10 million, for just a few weeks. Though disappointed, I was quick to agree and move on.

With this détente in place, my relationship with Fred healed somewhat, and we were able to work together. But Sovereign had taken a big hit; it was like a $10 million loan gone bad. The whole situation also hurt our reputation and standing in the investment banking community.

The boardroom intrigue restarted on another front. Out of the blue, Paul Wieand called to congratulate me on the bank's successes and asked to be put back on the board. In the interim, he had earned a Ph.D. in psychology, somewhat ironically focusing on emotional intelligence. I advocated on his behalf with the board to give him a seat. They balked at the idea. After all, we were trying to rebuild cohesiveness, and Paul had already been divisive. Indeed, allowing him back into the company ended up being a very poor decision on my part.

Paul decided he wanted to replace Fred as chairman of the board. There were many reasons not to allow that to happen, not least of which were Paul's modus operandi and my truce with Fred. Despite our differences, I respect what Fred accomplished in his turkey farming and warehouse businesses. There's actually a highway named for him now in Allentown.

I again turned to Joe Harenza at Stephens & Lee, who wrote a letter to Paul informing him of the board's decision not to renominate him to the bank's board. I felt sad that I had made Paul very angry once again, but I had to put our business interests before my friend's interest. With that unfortunate incident resolved, business went on. It was a relief and a pleasure to continue making acquisitions and building Sovereign.

I never ever gave up. Not when business was poor. Not when hobbled by a broken hip for several months. Not when boardroom drama boiled over. My persistence was rewarded and was about to lead me in exciting new directions.

Chapter 9

FROM BANKING TO PRIVATE EQUITY... AND BACK TO BANKS

For any company, a fractured board severely impedes the superb execution of the company's strategic vision. But the flip side is that alignment within the whole organization, including the board members and management team, is a key determinant of its success.

In the wake of the S&L crisis from 1989 to 1991, during my early years as CEO at Sovereign Bancorp, achieving complete alignment was pivotal to the bank's recovery. Our team, the invaluable human resources, was committed to the four critical success factors I've already discussed but that bear repeating, namely (1) high asset quality, (2) low-interest rate risk, (3) high productivity and low-efficiency ratios, and (4) exceptional service quality while emphasizing teamwork. This strategic focus eventually yielded exceptional results of a 20 percent plus/ minus average annual compounded growth rate for investors during the seventeen years I was the CEO at Sovereign.

My priority was to ensure alignment by engaging our team in authentic assessments of the current health and direction of Sovereign, including, "What is our strategy?" "Where are we heading?" "How are we going to get there?" "What are our strengths, weakness, and opportunities?" And "What external factors can impact us?"Everyone on the team had to agree on how to answer these questions consistently and unwaveringly. This alignment is only possible when senior management communicates transparently and accepts others' inputs willingly.

The power of an engaged team is unmatched, and that engagement requires passion, so having that drive was a primary criterion for being hired at Sovereign. Despite my positive professional development experiences at Harvard, Dartmouth, and YPO forums, I didn't seek candidates there. I preferred to work with people who were passionate and driven rather than individuals with extraordinarily high IQs who were unmotivated and unable to adapt.

So, how did Sovereign achieve the level of alignment necessary to ensure the superlative execution of our strategy? By empowering the management team. My leadership style was to model transparent communication by asking meaningful questions and listening intently to the answers. I facilitated offsite retreats every three to five months, and every senior executive had an opportunity to openly express their thoughts and opinions on our current state and future outlook. Spending time together *outside* the office served to foster an environment of personal and professional growth *inside* the office. Further, it unified the team to work together toward accomplishing a common mission.

Three main areas of alignment emerged from these meetings: (1) company growth must be in accordance with our critical success factors as opposed to growth simply for the sake of growth, (2) growth can stem from organic or external changes like mergers and acquisitions (M&A), and (3) *not* to focus on being everything to everyone but on being outstanding in a few areas. Focus, focus, focus on fewer products and fewer services, and do these few things very well rather than many in a mediocre way!

Besides the offsite sessions, I held onsite office "Ask Jay" small group meetings with various departments. This was another forum where I could communicate our strategic priorities, update everyone on the company's progress and top management's plans and get feedback. And I went a step further by supplementing these group sessions with individual meetings every six months.

At a meeting at one branch, someone shared an astonishing frustration. Every time the branch needed toilet paper, they had to complete a procurement request form. What a ridiculous bureaucratic procedure. The other senior executives and I became bureaucracy weed killers. But once you get rid of one unreasonable process or policy, another grows. It's a fact of organizational life that whenever three or more people are involved, a company becomes bureaucratic. However, Sovereign's senior executives stayed informed and took appropriate proactive measures, thus limiting the frequency and severity of administrative roadblocks.

Fortunately, my leadership efforts to improve our operations worked! We achieved alignment, our initiatives were executed, and our employees were happy. It's a testament to the bank's senior management that there was minimal staff turnover.

With our house in order, my role shifted primarily to growth opportunities through M&As as well as investor and shareholder relations. We needed capital and an effective stock price to accomplish the M&As. The goal was to create organic growth and facilitate superior execution of all the companies we were integrating to form a single high-performing company.

We devised a competitive edge. Most of our competitors were going after the better-performing companies and paying a premium for them. Instead, we targeted banks that weren't doing well but were in good markets with the potential to become high performing, much like we hired high-potential staff rather than complacent individuals. A limited number of entities went after those weaker banks, thus elevating our chances of success.

The other prong of our competitive M&A strategy was that, as CEO, I was responsible for all direct communication with the CEOs and boards of the desirable target companies. Most other banks relied on advisors, not leadership, for deal-making, so my personal involvement gave Sovereign an advantage. Company leaders appreciated interacting with me as the decision-maker. My approach at the meetings was to be 100 percent authentic. I would tell Sovereign's story from the Penn Saving days to the present and explain how we had identified their company as one with excellent growth potential. Armed with research and honesty, I would describe three or four strengths (what their company was doing well) before I'd discuss where we'd fit in and how, together, we'd overcome their weaknesses to ensure their future success.

This approach worked. We didn't close *all* the deals, but we achieved almost 90 percent of them. I derived great satisfaction in Sovereign's transformation from a pitifully failing bank to a major financial player. I loved every minute of the process, and I was tenacious. I had mastered my father's lessons of defining a mission and focusing on its execution. What applied to his military career also applied to every aspect of my life, including my business dealings.

I had many memorable interactions with bankers, investors, and shareholders, but one stands out in particular. Harmonia Bank in Kenilworth, New Jersey, was in my sights. It was a small suburban bank with solid potential and had approximately $1 billion in deposits, which was just the kind of bank I wanted. But I was told by other bankers that it was run by a difficult, autocratic guy who'd never agree to see me. What did I do? I never ever gave up. I went there one day without an appointment and told the CEO I was driving through the area and had heard about Harmonia. Surprisingly, he met with me. I told him I recognized that he was in a tough market and admired how he overcame challenges. Then, I asked him to tell me the story of how he built Harmonia and listened intently.

The banker didn't seem domineering as I had been forewarned. Instead, he was thrilled to meet with a peer to share how he built a stable bank, despite naysayers telling him it couldn't be done. In a subsequent meeting, we closed the deal. Our chairman at the time, Fred Jaindl, had bet me $100 that I couldn't close the deal. Fred never liked losing, and it felt great to get a crisp $100 bill from him at our next board meeting.

Sovereign's strategy of using personal relationships, especially on a CEO-to-CEO level, maximized the success of our M&A mission. When I assumed the helm of Sovereign, we had zero presence in the very ripe New Jersey market. By the early 2000s, we were the state's second-largest bank!

Closing deals and working with talented, passionate, and driven people energized me. I often thought, *why am I getting paid to have so much fun building a solid presence in the financial services industry*? Sovereign was thriving, and so was I. Sovereign made more than two dozen acquisitions during my tenure, including acquiring branches from Fleet Bank and Bank of Boston and became a major regional bank with branches from New Hampshire to Maryland.

Although new political boardroom distractions were on the horizon, I was still committed to taking the long view, but my vision for strengthening the bank was slowly being stymied by the board's machinations. It was a clear case of misalignment between the board and management. We were losing the focus I prized so highly and were blowing away tremendous opportunities. Ultimately, decisions I wholeheartedly disagreed with would turn a profitable, highly functional company into a dysfunctional mess. But I'm prematurely jumping to the end of my Sovereign story. There's a lot more to tell first.

Despite Sovereign's impressive bottom line, we began having problems with our investors and shareholders. Not everyone agreed with my focus on long-term strategy and execution. Some challenging times lay ahead for Sovereign and for me. The one constant in life is change, right?

Around 2003, I visited San Diego, California, and an investment banker suggested I meet with a hedge fund manager named Ralph Whitworth of Relational Investors. He was very gracious, and we had a pleasant conversation. That was that, at least, for then.

Several months later, Ralph was in Philadelphia on business and asked to meet with me. Ralph had prepared a booklet detailing his success in turning around Mattel and several other large companies. He made a zealous pitch about how he could help make similar major positive changes at Sovereign. My interest was piqued, and I carefully listened to his ideas. Ralph contended that we were giving up a lot of yield on loans and suggested we only focus on the highest-yielding loans. He argued that he could help Sovereign by charging higher prices for loans to improve revenues, as he had done for Mattel.

I responded politely but bluntly, "We are not Mattel. We have to worry about risk management. Our raw material is customer deposits, and our sales are loans." It was irrelevant to us that Mattel charged higher prices if a large group of customers couldn't pay, and loans would go bad. Yes, if Sovereign charged higher prices, we would make more money in the short term. However, if our customers couldn't repay us in full, we'd lose our shirt. In banking, one must ensure, first and foremost, that a loan will be paid back. I explained to Ralph that his proposal violated one of our main critical success factors, that of superior credit quality. Ralph was gung-ho, but I'm not easily intimidated. My "No" was unequivocal.

I remained confident that a long-term view was our best bet. Two trends had emerged, the Spanish population in the US was growing, and European markets had an increasingly prominent role in the US economy. The board directed me to identify a partner who could help us capitalize on these trends, especially with Hispanics.

I began to make contacts with the help of a few investment bankers and lay the groundwork for collaboration. I clicked with Emilio Botin, the CEO of Banco Santander in Madrid. He and I shared the same growth vision. Emilio told me stories of his time serving on the board of the Royal Bank of Scotland, and he was an authentic man. He didn't claim to be the smartest person in the room, but he was hungry to learn from others. I was impressed by the nature of his criticisms of the Royal Bank of Scotland, and his analysis was validated when the bank began having problems.

The timing was right for Sovereign to pursue a relationship with Banco Santander. We were looking at a huge acquisition opportunity in New York: Independence Community Bank. Sovereign could use Banco Santander's capital to develop a presence in the low-risk, multi-family businesses and solid deposit base in Brooklyn. There was also a growing Hispanic population in New York, and collaborating with Banco Santander would give us a strong entry position. It would be a win-win situation for all involved parties.

The Sovereign board agreed on the terms of the deal, and the company would greatly benefit from the capital infusion. In 2006, Banco Santander became a 19.9 percent shareholder with its equity investment. Further, the deal stipulated that they would have the option to acquire the rest of the company within five years at a 100 percent higher price than their original investment.

By capping Banco Santander's investment at 19.9 percent, we circumvented a major regulatory limitation, namely that the board of a publicly traded company requires shareholder consent for any common stock issuance of

20 percent or more. However, shareholder activism can cut through this safeguard.

Ralph Whitworth wasn't at all pleased with the Banco Santander deal because, as I've said, long-term financial thinking wasn't his style. Ralph began to threaten a proxy fight and went public with our disagreement. He organized a private meeting with the shareholders. In 2004, the drumbeats of war sounded. Ralph was a shareholder activist, an individual who used his partial stake in a publicly traded corporation to force significant change. He demanded that he sit in our boardroom and warned that if we didn't agree to his terms, he'd take further action. Although Sovereign offered Ralph a seat, we made it clear that we were sticking to our partnership strategy with Banco Santander, and besides, I really enjoyed my time serving on Banco Santander's board in Madrid.

At the second board meeting Ralph attended, I had mental flashbacks to the boardroom scene where Fred Jaindl banged the gavel years ago. Ralph literally stood on the boardroom table screaming vitriol; for example, he made unfounded accusations that Emilio Botin was involved in shady business concerns in Venezuela. I calmly responded to Ralph, saying that his behavior was inappropriate for a meeting and that if he had constructive comments, we'd listen and consider them. I told Ralph I had honored his request to be on the board, and, as CEO, I had affirmed our decision to make a deal with Banco Santander. I stood my ground. In front of everyone, Ralph said, "one of us has to go, and I'm telling you, it will be you, not me."

Ralph immediately began organizing shareholders, and less than two months later, he asked me to call a special board meeting in Philadelphia. Unsurprisingly, Ralph only had one item on the agenda: fire Jay. I said, "OK, but I'm a large shareholder, and expect you to honor your commitments to me." I also stated that I wanted it documented there and then that I believed Sovereign would be heading in the wrong direction by following his suggestions.

My heart and soul were invested in Sovereign, so I felt compelled to describe my recommendations for its future. The number one suggestion was to sell all the subprime mortgages and loans because, although they're high-yielding, they're also high-risk. I reminded the board that this strategy had been successful when we cleaned up other problem banks. Emilio Botin and another executive from Santander openly agreed with me. In the end, it didn't matter.

Ralph made a motion that Sovereign part company with me. December 31, 2006, was my last day at Sovereign. I walked away a very, very wealthy individual. Because I had a passionate attachment to Sovereign, I decided not to sell my stock. That was a huge mistake. Sometimes emotion obscures reality.

Within eighteen months, the new leadership took this high-performing growth company and turned it into a disaster.

Resilience means never ever giving up. Resilience allows individuals to turn a crisis into an opportunity. After twenty years at Sovereign, I explored the world by traveling, and I delved into business opportunities by networking.

I decided it was time to take a hiatus, shift gears, enjoy my family, and explore the world together. Together with my wife, Sherry, and children, Sam and Luvleen, I embarked on a worldwide whirlwind journey. Gone were the days of living on bread, milk, and vitamins. No more sleeping on railway platforms or dusty roads. This year-long adventure was the epitome of luxurious comfort, and unlike the trek from Delhi to London, this trip spanned Europe, Asia, and Australia, and we returned to North America over the Pacific.

My kids loved the experience. How could they not? Except for one stop. When we arrived in Dubai, the weather was typical, with sweltering temperatures hovering over 100 degrees. Sam and Luvleen weren't pleased, but I explained that authentic travel experiences are those when you live like the locals. Then, I reminded them we were staying in an airconditioned, top-notch hotel suite. It could be worse, and in life, you need to take some things in your stride and move onward.

It's clear from my adult children's behavior and the accomplishments in their personal and professional lives that I have imparted a core set of ethical values to them rooted in Sikhism, including an appreciation of their blessings. I can't miss this opportunity to digress and mention that, at one time, Sam and Luvleen were each running their own New York Stock Exchange publicly traded companies. I was told by the NYSE that this was the first time in its history that a father, daughter, and son were all in that esteemed position simultaneously. I'll expand on my children's careers later, but I couldn't resist sharing that achievement now. I am so very proud of my kids.

My career was at a turning point, and I knew I wouldn't stay away from the world of banking and finance for long. The travel hiatus re-energized me, and I decided to try a different sector of private equity. I established Sidhu Advisors, LLC, a private equity fund that collaborated with some larger firms, including Paulson & Co. Inc. John Paulson, the president and portfolio manager, and I discussed a joint effort to consult with problem banks and turn them around. But my partnership with John also fell apart. Despite signing a letter of intent, it was never executed after Lehman Brothers' failure.

In 2010, a beacon of light shone in The Sunshine State when the CEO of Atlantic Coast Financial in Jacksonville, Florida, called me out of the blue. He knew me by reputation and invited me to join the board of his troubled bank, hoping I'd help turn it around. Atlantic Coast had been established as a railroad employee credit union and transformed into a bank, but it had been all but decimated by the financial crisis.

I was ready for a challenge, and I owned a home about an hour from Jacksonville. The offer was appealing, and I accepted. After about three months, I felt like I'd gone back in time to when I first joined Penn Savings Bank. Atlantic Coast was a mutual bank that had recently turned public, and guess what they discussed in the boardroom? The same kind of trivial minutia that characterized Penn when I joined, including signage color, furniture, vacation time, and even personal affairs and divorces. All the while, they were bleeding money.

I invested $1 million of my depleted fortune in Atlantic Coast, and some contacts also invested, including my friend, Bhanu Choudhrie. I saw the company's potential and was confident that I could save the institution and turn it around, but it needed a wholesale change. I assumed a role I'd never performed. My position was summed up in a 2013 *Wall Street Journal* headline: "Sidhu Targets Atlantic Coast Makeover – Banker Tries Shareholder Activism For Change At Jacksonville Bank." Yes, I became an activist!

My first proposal was that the board and CEO at Atlantic Coast should be replaced. A swift, clean slate was required to resuscitate the bank. What did the board do? They decided to sell the company for $2 a share. Their initial equity offering had been for $10 a share, and that's what I had paid, five times more than their proposed sale price. My friend and co-investor, Bhanu Choudhie, had taken a board seat along with me. He and I were the only ones to vote against this ridiculous deal. So it went through.

Bhanu and I began a proxy fight, and the shareholders ultimately disapproved of the deal. It's not often that the board of directors announces an acquisition that is blocked by the shareholders. Within a year, the entire board was kicked out and replaced by a professional board and CEO. Then we made a deal to sell the company to Ameris Bancorp at a valuation five times higher than the $2 a share offer that Atlantic had been willing to accept.

It was now time for me to get back to doing what I do best and love most, running a company and being a dealmaker and change-maker!

Chapter 10

A NEW CENTURY... AND BEYOND

My foray into the private equity financial sector confirmed it isn't my forte; banking is my passion. I thrive on turning around failing banks and running them successfully and profitably. Unfortunately, Ralph Whitworth from Relational Investors had tried to impugn my character. But, despite the debacle that ensued when I was forced out of Sovereign Bank, I never gave up. Instead, I was resilient. That experience served to magnify my drive to restore my reputation and invigorated my passion for returning to the banking world. My friend Dick Ehst and others encouraged me to undertake another leadership role. Not just encouraged me; they said they'd join me.

Although it was 2009, a new century beckoned!

Ken Mumma was the Chairman and CEO of New Century Bank, headquartered in Phoenixville, Pennsylvania, and worked with his wife, Moira Forbes. Sadly, while dating Moira, Ken was in a car accident that left him paralyzed from the waist down. He's a very respectable, smart guy, but he simply couldn't put 100 percent of his energy into New Century Bank. So, he hired the head of private banking for CoreStates Bank to run it as its president. This individual tried to use private banking approaches with customers who were skilled trade entrepreneurs like plumbers and electricians, and the bank got into big trouble. Ken blindly trusted the president he'd hired and couldn't clearly see the mismanagement plaguing the company.

Several factors appealed to me about the opportunity to tackle and transform New Century Bank, including working with Ken, staying in the Pennsylvania area near Sovereign, and, best of all, a golden opportunity to make a small bank into a robust financial entity. Ken and I talked frankly about the situation, and I asked him to give me a week to diagnose the bank's ailments and prescribe a cure.

It may seem counterintuitive, but running a small bank is much more challenging than running a large one. The leadership needs to worry about every detail and every dollar, and banking is highly regulated by the US government. Several supervisory bodies oversee the financial industry, including the Federal Reserve Board (FRB), the Federal Deposit Insurance Corp. (FDIC), the State Department of Banking, and the Securities and Exchange Commission (SEC). So, before I invested time and money, I talked to the regulators and conditioned my investment on their allowing me the chance to acquire any failing banks in the area. They agreed, and we made a deal!

I did my homework and spent twelve-plus-hour days at the bank. While driving home through Pennsylvania's country roads, I calculated that New Century was losing an average of $12 thousand a day! I'd never before had brackets indicating negative numbers on an income statement. This was serious!

I enlisted several former Sovereign colleagues and trusted friends, including Dick Ehst, to collectively invest $17 million in New Century with me. And with Dick's invaluable input, I put together a plan. I told Ken that the current president had to go, and I needed to bring in my own management team. Ken heartily endorsed the arrangement and remained a director while I became chairman and CEO. He also agreed to bring in Dick as president and COO.

We engineered a three-pronged strategy that was well executed by our highlyqualified and experienced executive team. To make New Century healthy, we proposed to (1) generate revenues through high-quality variable-rate loans, (2) cut costs and make the bank more efficient, and (3) fix the loan problems ASAP. We launched a new mortgage warehouse division, spearheaded by Glen Hedde, to bring in high quality variable-rate loans quickly to build the revenue stream. Mortgage warehousing provides short-term funding to loan originators. The underlying mortgages are then sold by the originators on the secondary market. This financing enabled the bank to develop expertise in a niche that provides solid recurring revenues from high-quality loans and fees.

My first six to twelve months at New Century were tiring but inspiring. The regulators were true to their word and allowed us to take over two small failing banks. With the support of the FDIC, we made around $40 million in bargain purchase gains. I'm grateful that the FDIC permitted us, a private enterprise, to turn around banks for less money than the government would spend. Within eighteen months, New Century was earning at least $10 to $12 thousand a day. What a massive swing from losing $12 thousand a day!

It was rewarding to me that, in the beginning, the new management team at New Century was comprised of many former Sovereign colleagues, including our new President and Chief Operating Officer, Chief Financial Officer, Chief Banking Officer, and Head of Small Business. This level of loyalty and trust was crucial to achieving the strategic alignment that drove our success. Not only is it wonderful for the leadership to share the same principles, values, and strategic focus, but it is also wonderful to work with friends who are committed to a common vision.

I often reflect on the role of a leader and always look back on the lessons my father taught me. Four fundamental requirements are essential for an effective leader at any level of an organization. The leader must (1) have a clear vision, mission, goals, and strategic plan to achieve those goals with alignment throughout the organization, (2) master their internal environment through authentic self-assessment of strengths and areas for improvement, (3) master their external environment, i.e., how are the economy, competition, and customer needs, etc., changing and impacting performance, and (4) be passionate about continual improvement. All this requires focus. It comes down to being proactive and agile in the face of change, persevering despite obstacles, and passionately seeking continuous improvement. Other requirements for effective leadership include eliminating any bureaucracy that impedes progress and being obsessed with creating a customer-centric company.

Banking is among the most antiquated, slow-moving industries in the US. It began as a family cottage industry. Being local meant the board of directors was usually comprised of local realtors, insurance agents, and land developers, not professional businesspeople. But as banks became less localized and went public, they needed experts who could think outside the box, pivot when necessary, and think about their roles in terms of the factors I've described above.

I've talked a lot about failing banks, and you may wonder how banks could possibly fail. After all, the equation for success seems easy and foolproof. The bank takes in money, pays low interest, and loans it at higher interest rates. How could this get messed up by a bank?

Let me compare banks to manufacturing companies. A bank's raw material is cash that comes in the form of deposits. The products we manufacture from that raw material (cash) are loans. So there is a simple principle in business: raw material costs and processing expenses have to be less than what you sell your product for, and there must be a market for your product. As the S&L crisis demonstrated, many banks failed because they ignored this principle. Instead, they paid more for deposits and operating expenses than their revenue. That was the recipe for failure.

It is also critical for banks to manage their credit risk to get their loans repaid to make a profit. Failing banks forget to operate with a positive operating margin. In addition, successful banks have strong risk management principles, run their banks efficiently, and are customer-centric and forward-thinking.

The banking industry is also characterized by tough regulation and a permanent need for capital. That combination means you must show profits to satisfy both the regulators and your investors. Additionally, there are big players in the financial industry like Bank of America and JP Morgan Chase, so smaller banks must find a focus to establish their unique identity, their niche.

New Century Bank became Customers Bancorp in 2010 (the name reflects its emphasis on people) and has grown from $250 million in assets to a $20 billion asset bank holding company today. It trades on the New York Stock Exchange as CUBI. It has developed from a local Chester Country, Southeastern Pennsylvania bank with a few branches to a national company at the forefront of digital banking. Its forward-thinking embrace of fintech has led to an annual income and asset growth rate of about forty-four percent. Not bad for a bank!

Customers Bancorp is carving out its niche; it's not a giant, but neither is it a midget. It has examined its internal capabilities and external conditions and trends and determined that it is a customer-centric business bank with a highly experienced young team, strong risk management principles, and tech-savvy forward-thinking strategies to "wow" customers. This is a winning combination. Consumer banking had been dependent on branch networks. In contrast, Customers is not branch-centric, and its consumer banking is conducted through digital technologies.

When my daughter Luvleen was studying for her bachelor's degree at Harvard University, she came to me with a brilliant idea to incubate a consumer bank that attracts college students by using digital technologies like smartphones and tablets. Tapping this young market was effective for many reasons, and students generally stick with their first bank for life. (I still use the VISA credit card issued to me as a student!) Luvleen subsequently earned an MBA at The Wharton School at the University of Pennsylvania.

The result of Luvleen's entrepreneurial vision was BankMobile, which partners with universities and large businesses to help market and support their products. Then Customers Bank spun off BankMobile to become BM Technologies, which went public in 2021. Its symbol on the NYSE is BMTX. BankMobile was the first bank in the US to wipe out overdraft fees and other similar nuisance fees, bringing the attention of the public to an industry-wide problem, namely that banks were charging billions of dollars of fees each year that not only cost consumers but yielded inefficient branch returns. Now, the "big four banks" (Bank of America, JP Morgan Chase, Wells Fargo, and Citibank) are following suit. This no-fee policy reflects the trend to accelerate the closing of bank branches. Why? They depend on high fees to cover their excessive real estate, personnel, and other ancillary carrying costs.

While BM Technology focuses on consumer banking, Customers Bancorp concentrates on business banking. When I was in my 60s, I had no plans to retire, but I did want to think about succession planning for Customers. Our board takes corporate governance very seriously, and they also thought it prudent to bring someone new on board. Dick was in charge of the search and hired a recruitment firm to look both internally and outside the organization for his and my successors. Our primary criterion was to find tech-savvy leaders with significant experience in the financial services industry who shared our vision and values, people capable of leading Customers for the next couple of decades.

Dick announced at a board meeting that he'd found an ideal candidate: Sam Sidhu. I was flabbergasted at the suggestion that my son should take over. Yes, Sam was well-educated, with a Wharton School degree in economics and a Harvard MBA. Yes, Sam was trustworthy, and his values and vision were compatible with ours. Yes, he had a stellar resume, but there was one pitfall. Sam had founded his own private equity firm, Megalith Capital Management, in New York. I felt sure Sam wouldn't leave the firm he'd established with a Harvard classmate over ten years ago. He was as passionate about his work as I was about mine!

I expressed my doubts to Dick, not about Sam's qualifications but his willingness. And Dick responded with my mantra, "I never ever give up!" They met a few times and invited me to join them at The Radnor Hotel near Philadelphia for dinner one evening. Sam said he'd consider the offer but wouldn't make a commitment right away. He said he'd be walking away from a large investment in time, money, and people. And a lot of income.

I was impressed that Sam said he would want to bring his partner Phil Watkins into Customers and that he'd want equity. It reminded me of when I was enticed by equity when I joined Penn Savings Bank. Sam also said he'd need a few years to properly shut down his fund. When Sam decided to join us as Chief Operating Officer of Customers Bank in January 2020, he brought along his Harvard classmate to run our commercial real estate business.

Then, COVID hit. Congress passed the CARES Act in March 2020 to fund programs to mitigate the financial impact of COVID. The Small

Business Association (SBA) backed loans to finance the Paycheck Protection Program (PPP), which loaned money to small- and medium-sized businesses. The goal was to keep their workforce employed and their business afloat. These folks were our customers, and they needed our help. They were facing an emergency, so the loans needed to be distributed quickly, efficiently, and in accordance with government policies and practices.

Customers Bancorp would receive an administrative fee for our services, and I told the board we could make about $45 million. Sam was even more optimistic, saying, "What if we made $100 million?" Others thought we were crazy; maybe we'd make $4 million at best. How could we compete with the big banks that had hundreds of branches and thousands of employees?

We partnered with other companies without bank charters but which were digitally connected to small businesses. We tapped into Application Programming Interface (API) connectivity, a software program that handles data transfers. We were combining our banking expertise with cutting-edge technology! The result was we distributed more Paycheck Protection loans than Bank of America, totaling $400 million in revenues over two years. As to the individual who cautioned we'd only make $4 million and was proved wrong? He acknowledged his thinking was too traditional, and our thinking was outside the box. He became a champion of the new way to distribute PPP loans and became head of all our community banking, including Small Business Administration (SBA) lending.

Most significantly, by distributing PPP funds, we saved about three million jobs and developed relationships with about 300,000 small businesses across America! I still hear small business owners express their appreciation for our accessibility and assistance that enabled them to survive during desperate times.

I'm proud of the legacy we're building, especially our resilience. The future of Customers Bank is very bright. We have a superb management team, the best I've ever worked with in my entire career. I'm excited about our succession plans and our continued growth and success.

As for me, it might seem odd, but I want the very last check that I write in my life to bounce. Why? Because it would mean that I've lived my life fully, and it would mean that my children have secured financial success on their own through their hard work, entrepreneurial spirit, focus, and impeccable ethics. What more could a parent want?

Chapter 11

GIVING BACK

It's certainly gratifying to feel that you've positively impacted your children's lives. It's also wonderful to feel that you've contributed to the future of the financial services industry, although, admittedly, it's also incredible to have earned a significant sum of money in the process. However, it's an entirely different privilege to have an opportunity to make a difference in the lives of thousands of future leaders.

More than thirty years after I arrived in Wilkes-Barre with my few possessions and slept alongside homeless seniors in a YMCA until Wilkes University reopened for the semester, I was given that chance.

In 2004, my alma mater, Wilkes University, honored me by renaming its business school the "Jay S. Sidhu School of Business and Leadership." What's more, they allowed me to participate in redesigning the school's curriculum. My involvement in rebranding the school allowed me to share what I've learned about professional and personal growth with the next generation of aspiring business leaders. My time at Wilkes meant a great deal to me, and this was my chance to give back.

Wilkes was founded in 1933 and was initially located on a satellite campus of the highly-ranked Bucknell University. Now, its state-of-the-art facilities are situated on its own thirty-five-acre campus. The school is named after John Wilkes, an English 18th-century politician who advocated for free speech, individualism, religious tolerance, and other liberties. Fittingly, Wilkes-Barre, a progressive city with industrial beginnings, carries his name too. In recent years, Wilkes University has enjoyed impressive growth, with a current total enrollment of over 5,200 students in its undergraduate and graduate schools. The Wilkes team is rightfully proud of its liberal arts roots and burgeoning graduate schools. I wanted the rebranding of the business school to complement and build upon that history.

In the years leading up to 2004, I had been talking with Bob Capin, the professor who had encouraged me to read all of General Electric's public SEC filings as a first-year student. That exercise was a valuable way to learn authentically about accounting and management. Bob was Wilkes University's president from 1975 to 1984 and was subsequently named its first president emeritus.

Bob Capin and I had several discussions about possible ways I could become more engaged at Wilkes. Upon Bob's retirement, Chris Breiseth became Wilkes' fourth president, and he and I continued discussing how I could help the university achieve its vision. Both Bob and Chris invited me to join the board of trustees, but at the time, I felt I was too busy building Sovereign to devote the time the role merited.

In 2001, Tim Gilmour, a real visionary leader, was named Wilkes's fifth president, and I agreed to join the board of trustees shortly thereafter. Tim proposed to me the idea of changing the school's Department of Commerce to the School of Business. That's when he offered me naming rights to the school. I insisted we make it a unique program to develop future leaders for the region and the ever-changing world.

Tim invited me to participate in Wilkes' business school curriculum development and asked for my thoughts on how business and leadership were evolving. We discussed in-depth how universities could better prepare students for their future business endeavors in light of the changing business landscape. I told Tim that universities had to do a better job of creating value. If you're going to build a quality business school, I suggested, it must be *leadership and industry-focused*. There has to be a sense of what businesses need in this world of global interconnectedness. Yes, I said, schools must teach the fundamentals, including math, economics, corporate finance, managerial accounting, and so on, but equally important are the skills that make great thinkers, leaders, and innovators. *That* is what would create value for Wilkes graduates.

When Tim Gilmour and I considered the curriculum for what would become the Sidhu School, I again insisted on a few things. For example, it had to have a leadership training element with a full-scale, all-encompassing leadership training focus. It must also offer a personal development component and a post-graduate mentorship program. At the time, these were revolutionary ideas.

As we developed the school and its curriculum, Tim shared my strategic vision for leading Wilkes University into the future. Around this time, a good buddy of mine, Jack Miller, took over as chairman of the board of trustees, and two years after his term, I became the chairman. During that time, Jack and I grew very close (he later became a trusted board member at Customers Bancorp). We often knew each other's thoughts without speaking. I sensed that he and I were poised to make something great happen at Wilkes University. We called it an "action-based approach" to teaching, with conceptual learning supported by real-world marketing and practical business projects.

Jack and I both felt we needed to hire faculty who understood that education is constantly changing and what is essential for students to learn in today's and tomorrow's economic environments, faculty who understood the importance of meaningful experiential learning using innovative methodologies. We knew we needed to provide a variety of courses in diverse areas of expertise to keep pace with current market trends. Our most significant job was to prepare students to succeed in the real world. That's what the true value of an education means.

In addition to offering undergraduate degrees in entrepreneurship, finance, management, marketing, and sports management, the Sidhu School has an accelerated degree completion option for adult learners and a Bachelor of Science degree with a major in accounting. Minors are offered in accounting, entrepreneurship, finance, leadership, management, and marketing. The curriculum also focuses on mentoring, emotional intelligence, and honest communication. Currently, under the leadership of Dean Abel Adekola, we have developed a value-based approach to authentic leadership, namely the development of the *whole* individual.

As part of the focus on the qualities of whole, well-rounded individuals, students are exposed to several pillars of business leadership as they pursue their degrees. Our list of core values is long and comprises learner focus, innovation, scholarship, diversity, market relevance, societal impact, integrity, personal development, continuing education, and community service. It's an expansive but achievable vision.

Learner focus – an emphasis on the whole person to enhance the individual's personal and professional development with one-on-one mentoring.

Innovation – an environment that fosters creativity and independent, outside-the-box thinking.

Scholarship – a rigorous course of study that insists on intellectual contributions that advance knowledge.

Diversity –a commitment to social awareness and responsibility, a global perspective, and a diverse student body.

Relevance – an exploration of the application of theories and concepts that are relevant to evolving trends and business practices.

Integrity – a focus on authenticity and ethical behavior as the cornerstones of healthy societies, economies, and relationships.

Continuing education – a recognition that learning continues in educational opportunities beyond the classroom.

Personal development – a concentration on the personal attributes like self-awareness, compassion, and high emotional intelligence (EQ) that drive meaningful and successful lives.

Community service – a commitment to social awareness and social action.

In addition to the coursework, Wilkes students complete a social action and community service project each year. Many local programs have benefitted from this participation, including the YMCA, a domestic violence center, the Humane Society, and a local food bank.

The Sidhu School also has a unique requirement of the Personal and Professional Development Series, a developmental advising and coaching program that helps students achieve their potential. Every undergraduate in the Sidhu School, no matter their major, takes part in this series, which grounds them in the basics of emotional intelligence, including self-awareness, empathy, and integrity. These qualities are all cultivated at the school not just as ideals but as achievable goals.

President Gilmour once told me he had experienced resistance to our priorities. He reported that many people asked him why anyone should take courses like this in a business school. Well, those people didn't realize that it's not just about skills anymore. Many other factors determine one's success in business. So much has changed that business education has to change as well.

The Sidhu School has always stressed leadership training along with traditional education. Classes are important, but you can take an Economics 101 course online; you cannot learn *leadership* online. Learning leadership skills requires face-to-face interaction and a real focus. That being said, students need to be educated on how cutting edge-technological advances are creating a new global landscape and require new ways of adapting and progressing.

The simple step of requiring all first-year students to take a leadership class was a game changer for the school. After Tim left Wilkes, I helped the university recruit another visionary leader, Patrick F. Leahy, to be the sixth president of the university. He believed the leadership course would make Wilkes's business education truly unique. As I explained to the administration, authentic leadership is not something one is usually born with; it needs to be taught and practiced. We need to help students become more well-rounded individuals so they can tackle any kind of problem in any kind of situation.

In 2014, President Leahy marked the tenth anniversary of Sidhu School's founding by cutting the ribbon to the business school's new $3 million building. This building offers numerous valuable tools for students, including a trading classroom with a stock ticker and classrooms with video conference capabilities. The new school also has the capacity for 600 graduate and undergraduate students. Previously, classes were scattered across three buildings around the campus. This consolidation facilitates all-important collaboration and networking with peers.

In 2017, a new major in hospitality leadership was added for students interested in careers in hotels, resorts, restaurants, tourism, event marketing and operation, and gaming and casino management. Electives include special topics in international tourism.

About eighteen months ago, I visited Wilkes for a terrific interactive forum with Patrick Leahy before he left Wilkes for another position in front of a huge audience of students at the university's McHale Athletic Center. We discussed a variety of topics, including the importance of passion about what you do, the difference between leadership and management, the current and future technological revolutions, the crucial pursuit of innovation, the need to make complex things simple, the importance of leadership, and of never giving up on your vision and mission.

All those issues were at the forefront when Customers Bancorp was created. Launched as a business-only bank, it also incubated BankMobile, a bank with no branches, which now has 1.7 million customers across the United States. Customers Bank has become a fast-growing, highly profitable, digital, and technology-forward business bank with about $20 billion in deposits.

The Jay S. Sidhu School of Business and Leadership's curriculum stresses having a vision for the success of a business, knowing what your mission is, and identifying the steps necessary to achieve it. These principles have been important to me throughout my life, and now they are equipping new generations of students to thrive and contribute to the business world.

The new Wilkes president, Greg Cant, is another great visionary, and he and Dean Adekola are passionate about taking the school to the next level. They are combining the Business School with the School of Engineering, making both leadership and technology the core competencies and unique features of these educational programs. I'm looking forward to further supporting them in their future endeavors.

Like the Jay S. Sidhu School, I'm moving forward into the future, where innovation and passion are going to be more crucial than ever.

Chapter 12

THE VALUES I LIVE BY

Being authentic, always standing up for what is true and right, the equality of all human beings, and giving to others in need, regardless of their sex, religion, race, national origin, or creed, are the central tenets of Sikhism. It's not simply a religion but a way of life. My commitment to these principles infuses every facet of my life, including my business relationships and leadership philosophy.

My parents were deeply spiritual, and every Sunday growing up, my family went to the gurdwara, not only to meditate and listen to God's words but also to perform deeds of public service. Gurdwaras worldwide, not just in India, welcome anyone at any time. They also provided me with spiritual comfort, rest, and sustenance on several occasions during my hitchhiking trip long ago.

Sharing food is a communal expression of hospitality, and my mother, and later Sherry, would prepare food that we'd buy or bring from home and help serve it at the gurdwara. A traditional vegetarian meal, langar, is served communally. Sitting on the floor and eating the same food symbolizes the equality of all people. It's a beautiful, spiritual, and delicious experience! Even as a young boy, I felt a deep connection with Sikh rituals. Each day in India alone, Sikh gurdwaras feed about ten million people of all backgrounds.

In Indian culture, when people show up, either invited or uninvited, the hosts insist that everyone is fed. If you've ever watched a portrayal of or attended an Indian wedding, you've seen how elaborate it is, overflowing with food, music, and dancing. The joy and abundance are incredible!

Hospitality is just one of the many values that reflect Sikhism's emphasis on sharing, giving, and helping others. To be truly meaningful, you must perform acts of loving kindness without expecting anything in return. The satisfaction of giving is its own reward. This concept is expressed by the word "seva," which means "selfless service," and perfectly encapsulates the overarching vision of Sikhism.

Seva's meaning is echoed in the motto "Service Above Self" of the Rotary International Club, an organization that had a profound impact on me. I was an active Interactor and Rotaractor in high school and college and was grateful to be on the receiving end of the group's generosity back when I traveled through Teheran as a kid. I met with a group of Rotarian businessmen, and the owner of a bus company gave us free bus tickets to Istanbul. It was a much-appreciated gift on my journey to promote peace among nations.

I learned from Rotary International leaders and from other mentors that leaders contribute and inspire by their behavior and action, not by words and empty promises. Put another way, *doing* is more powerful than *saying.* My parents modeled the value of community engagement and philanthropy, and I've tried to instill my commitment to social action in my children, Sam and Luvleen.

Here's the overarching principle by which I live my life and run my businesses: *The best leaders are those who are the best human beings. They are emotionally, spiritually, and intellectually mature and fulfilled, whatever their definition of fulfillment or happiness may be.*

Every year, our family would visit India to deepen our relationships with relatives and strengthen the children's link to our culture and the importance of giving. In high school, Sam and Luvleen each planned and implemented impressive community service projects to positively impact Indians' lives. Like my father and me, they learned the value of fulfilling a selfless mission.

One of Sam's projects was developing a computer center for needy people at a time when computers were not readily available in India. With help from an uncle, he took the project from conception to implementation. By talking to locals, he identified the schools where he set up the computers. The program was a big success. While Sam was a student at Penn, he even took several Wharton School students and faculty with him to visit the centers.

Luvleen was interested in women's health; she thought she'd go to medical school at one point but later decided to pursue business. In any event, she was deeply concerned about improving women's health. She interviewed doctors who confirmed women's medical care in India was woefully inadequate. Like Sam, Luvleen followed through on her vision and set up a four-week camp staffed by volunteers to address health problems.

As a family, we all became involved in a project inspired by my hitchhiking experience in Zurich. It's amazing that my trip had such a lasting impression and motivated many of my adult activities! I remembered a park in Zurich littered with needles discarded by addicts. There are many such parks in Reading, Pennsylvania, and we enlisted as many volunteers as possible to help clean up the garbage throughout the city. Our entire family, including the children, participated.

The Sikh principle of volunteering to help those in need by doing good deeds is paired with the core value of charitable giving. Like many faiths, Sikhism advocates donating about ten percent of your income, and Sherry and I are committed to philanthropy. From day one of my job at First Valley Bank, I gave what money I could.

At that time, I learned about the United Way, a network of local fund-raising affiliates. Always intellectually curious, I researched the organization and loved how it touches diverse local communities irrespective of religion, creed, caste, color, or gender. It's an expansive program with a mission to promote education, financial stability, and healthcare.

One year, Sherry and I were very privileged to be asked to chair the United Way capital campaign, which enabled us to visit every United Way-funded organization and beneficiary. We also visited businesses, labor unions, and other entities to enlist their cooperation. This is what it means to be a leader in life and in business: to inspire others to collaborate and contribute to the common good.

I strongly agree with Winston Churchill's statement, "We make a living by what we get. We make a life by what we give." In addition to the United Way, I became involved in spearheading fundraising campaigns for a diverse group of organizations in my local community, including Kutztown University, the Boys and Girls Club, a homeless shelter, a home for battered women, the YMCA, the Hispanic Chamber of Commerce, the Jewish Community Center, the Indian American Society, and the Caron Foundation for addiction treatment. Sherry is my partner in these endeavors. She is passionate about the Caron Foundation and actively participates in its various committees. Sherry's degree in psychology and healthcare makes her particularly well-suited to the organization. She also serves on the boards of several community organizations.

My choice of diverse organizations is intentional; it's fundamental to my belief that my job is to help *anyone* in need, regardless of background or status. I've received many honors and awards, but that isn't my purpose. The plaques and trophies are not on display. I'm simply humbled to have received them. The more you contribute, the more personal satisfaction you receive.

As I've said, leadership is about living your values through your actions. I hope my life story demonstrates the enormous significance I place on education. Like my brother and cousin, I had long dreamed of coming to America to get the best possible business education, and I did! The MBA I earned at Wilkes University launched my career in finance. Both my children are Ivy League educated and made use of their educations to become business pioneers.

In keeping with my commitment to contribute to the community I live in, I've contributed to local colleges, including Kutztown University, Albright College, Alvernia University, Penn State, Lycoming College, and Reading Area Community College. Of course, the Sidhu School of Business and Leadership at Wilkes University is exceptionally dear to me. It gave me so much as a student, and I'm delighted I'm in a position to give back as a graduate. Further, Wilkes University holds special meaning because it attracts many first-generation American students.

Continuing education throughout your life is of paramount importance. It's easy to find learning opportunities; you don't need to look far for exceptional programs. I'm very grateful for what I've learned at the Young Presidents' Organization (YPO) and its forums, Dartmouth, Wharton, and Harvard Business School. Remember that learning is not limited to a formal classroom; you can learn anywhere from anyone. And learn from your mistakes. I've made many, and I don't beat myself up about them. I learn from them and move forward. I know I'll make another mistake but, hopefully, it won't be the same one.

My personal and professional experiences have led me to think deeply about the qualities of a good leader. Great business leaders must promote a corporate culture that embraces the same principles that adults must embrace to be great human beings and to create healthy families. To be innovative, a company must focus on its people, collaboration, cooperation, and mutual trust and understanding.

Being a leader means having the responsibility for motivating and inspiring others, including you, who've taken the time to read this book. Also, I have the responsibility of demonstrating my philosophy through my actions. It means setting an example. To do so effectively, it's necessary to cultivate your EQ or emotional intelligence. Leadership requires the interpersonal skills inherent in respecting others, listening very carefully, taking their points of view into account, and communicating in a constructive manner. Great leaders are great human beings who have strengths in IQ and EQ, who are adaptable, and who are committed to continuous lifelong learning.

An additional attribute of a great leader is authenticity, to have empathy, be an active listener, be trusting and respectful, be there for others in need, and honestly say what you mean and do what you say. These principles were also behind my earliest leadership efforts when I spoke to Prime Minister Indira Gandhi, the Rotarians, and others to help realize my travel mission.

I've been honored to be invited to speak about authentic leadership, emotional intelligence, the future of banking, and business trends like artificial intelligence, technology, and electronic banking. I've made speeches all over the world, including in Dubai, Hong Kong, London, Prague, Sydney, and Delhi, and at Harvard, Wharton, and MIT, as well as several YPO universities and chapters in the US.

What do I talk about? Using my life experiences and stories, I discuss the many human qualities of a great leader I've mentioned above, including emotional intelligence, authenticity, humility, innovative thinking, hard work, respect, and the pursuit of self-improvement. And the number one quality is to be *authentic and passionate* about what you do!

I've followed my dream, and you can follow yours! We're blessed to live in America, an exceptional country that still is the land of opportunity, where you can rise above humble beginnings and achieve great things. Where there are equal opportunities for all. Where you are valued based on your performance. I remain optimistic, despite the political divisions and government dysfunction that are infecting the US today. We have great gifts to give to our people and the world. We can and will return to fulfilling our pledge of "liberty and justice for all."

How will America achieve its foundational principles again? Through exceptional *leadership*.

Chapter 13

MY FAMILY, AND OTHER SOURCES OF INSPIRATION

My mother turned 92 this year, while Sherry's mother is only two years away from 100! Sherry and our adult children, Sam and Luvleen, and their families recently went to India to celebrate Sherry's mother's 98th birthday. Imagine how special that family occasion was! Every year since Sherry has lived in the US, she has traveled to India to visit family. Even after Sam and Luvleen were born, Sherry would take them, at first, sitting in the economy section of Pan Am for the twenty-hour flight. This is a powerful example of our family's closeness and mutual respect.

Guru Granth Sahib, the holy scripture of Sikhism, says in a verse, "If you honor your parents, your parents will honor you." I've spoken at length about the high esteem I felt for my parents. My father's lessons on defining your mission and the steps to achieve it have indelibly affected and inspired me. He gave me the confidence to follow through on his advice. I envisioned driving his military Jeep as a young boy, and I did. I envisioned going to the US to attend business school and make money, and I did. I envisioned a loving, lifelong marriage and healthy children, and I am blessed.

Of course, there are also events that are beyond envisioning. Neither Sherry nor I imagined that one day, Sam, Luvleen, and I would achieve a historic feat of a son, daughter, and father, all serving as CEOs of NYSE publicly traded companies. I attribute my children's successful personal and professional lives equally to their upbringing and luck.

Our marriage, like most, has had its ups and downs. Still, we've always been committed to cultivating and strengthening our relationship and raising our children with solid core values. Our families have known each other for more than a generation. My and Sherry's dads were college and army buddies, and numerous other family connections exist between us. When I lived in the US as a young man and visited India, I enjoyed spending time with her family. Sherry is six years younger than me, and I was particularly friendly with her elder sister, who is about my age. Still, I'm blessed that Sherry was the woman who became my loving wife and life partner.

I had asked my mom to arrange a meeting with Sherry on one of my visits after my dad passed away. We didn't have an extended courtship, but there was a spark, and I proposed marriage. It's common for Indian marriages to be arranged this way. In the US, couples think they need to date for a long time or live together before they get married. That's not a guarantee of a successful marriage. An arranged marriage requires a special level of commitment to make the relationship work, and maybe that extra investment is a predictor of success. Indians have among the lowest divorce rates in the world!

When I proposed, Sherry hesitantly asked if I planned to return to India because she was very reluctant to leave her family. I promised her I'd do whatever she thinks is best for us, but right now, I was determined to earn at least $10,000 in the US before returning to India. She accepted my proposal, asking for reassurance that I'd have an open mind. She worried that she'd be unhappy so far away from her family. And initially, she did miss them terribly.

We got married in 1978 and settled in Bucks County, Pennsylvania. I wish my father had been at the wedding; he was quite fond of Sherry.

After the wedding, I made a huge mistake. Sherry and I had talked about taking a brief honeymoon, but the honeymoon never happened. My cousin, who, along with my brother, had inspired me to come to America, invited me to visit for my few remaining vacation days, and I did. (It took Sherry about twenty-five years to forgive me for that poor decision.) My priorities were misplaced; I should have prioritized my new wife. I learned a valuable lesson, to always invest in my marriage and family. Our son Sam was born in 1983, and our daughter Luvleen was born in 1986, and they've been our pride and joy.

Sherry and my values are 100 percent aligned on the subject of parenting.

We were committed to doing everything in our power to ensure our children were emotionally, spiritually, and intellectually healthy and, hopefully, better than their parents. Additionally, we strove to instill a passion for lifelong learning. Nevertheless, we understood that luck is also involved in rearing healthy, morally grounded children. We did the best we could, and by all measures, we did OK.

I credit Sherry for the lion's share of the childrearing. She gave up her career as a management trainee at Prudential and stayed at home as a full-time mother while I worked ferociously long hours and traveled on business. Our joint goal of raising the kids to be emotionally, spiritually, and intellectually mature was the predominant driver of our decision that Sherry would be the children's primary caregiver. Plus, my banking career was taking off.

I would sometimes bring Sam and Luvleen to the office on weekends, and many times, they traveled with me to offsite retreats. Whether it involved Sam and Luvleen meeting board members or business associates or stuffing envelopes, they were both exposed to the business world. I don't think their choice of careers in finance is entirely coincidental, and I don't think their success is coincidental either.

❁❁❁

Who doesn't want happy children? Who doesn't want successful children? Who doesn't want happy, successful children?

The million-dollar question is, "How do you instill the fundamental values that characterize mature, authentic, humane human beings?" The answer is there's no single magic formula, but there are ways to maximize the likelihood of succeeding.

The child's age matters, so start early. According to the University of Colorado, Boulder's sociologist Morris Massey, there are three stages of value development: (1) the imprint period up to age seven, when we absorb everything around us, (2) the modeling period between eight and thirteen, when we copy others' behavior, and (3) the socialization period between thirteen and twenty-one when we're influenced by peers and, increasingly, media.[1] Massey contends that the parents' influence is paramount until age thirteen, after which peers become more significant.

Maybe you're wondering how an academician's theory could be remotely helpful to you. Massey's paradigm of children's moral development underscores a simple truth that parents and grandparents can have an enormous impact on children's value systems and personal qualities throughout their childhood and teenage years. It's a short window of opportunity, so make good use of it. Give your kids the chance to learn, through living, what you consider essential. After all, you are their primary role model.

Another good question is, "What and who are the source of your value system?" Parents and grandparents are the first teachers, so it's up to you to determine what qualities you want to nurture. I hear my father's voice echoing focus, focus on your mission. Sherry's and my mission was to impart the message of being the best you can be and never giving up, being resilient, and persevering. As Steven Covey said, tough times don't last, but tough people do. These are the attitudes and behaviors we tried to demonstrate through our actions.

Additionally, we anchored our family life in our gurdwara, where we met other Indian families. We wanted to imbue the children with the Sikh principles of equality and respect, so connecting them to their culture was highly important to us, as was exposing them to diverse cultures. We prioritized developing spirituality and emotional maturity, along with intellectual capabilities. That was our definition of successful parenting.

To figure out *your* definition of what makes for successful children and how you'll get there, think of a few people you admire, like family members, leaders, teachers, and coaches. Then, think about their traits. *Why* do you admire them? Find three or four qualities and use them as a guidepost for building individuals with the tools to form authentic relationships and live authentic lives.

When I think about the people whom I admire most, besides my mother

---

[1] http://changingminds.org/explanations/values/values_development.htm

and father, I think about my YPO forum "brothers," colleagues, and friends like Dick Ehst and Dan Rothermel. Why? They inspire trust. They are caring and authentic and great listeners. They are successful yet humble. As a result, they inspire me to emulate them. And real, lifelong friends are the people you may not see for ten years, but when you do, you feel as if no time has elapsed. You feel as close as ever.

You saw in Massey's model that the centrality of adults in the lives of children shifts to peers in the teen years. Friends begin to influence them more than parents or other adults. We can't control our teens' behavior outside the house, but we can impart values early on that impact their decision-making and choices of friends. Sherry and I are so lucky in that both Sam and Luvleen's best friends now are the same kids they met when they were five years old! And their parents are also among our best friends, even today.

Another critical influence is your children's friend's parents. They, like you, affect their children's behavior. Get to know the parents of your children's friends. Make time to get together with them as families. This way, you can have input into who your children view as admirable role models.

Morris Massey also has many valuable insights into business and leadership, as he holds an MBA and Ph.D. in business. At First Valley Bank and Horizon Bank, a book by Massey was required reading for our salespeople to better understand the customers' perspectives. Just like a parent is responsible for instilling a healthy family culture, a business leader is also responsible for creating a respectful company environment.

I treasure each of my family members, and I've been remiss in not talking before now about my sister. She's fifteen years younger than me, and my mom called her the "unexpected addition." A happy addition, she's the light of our family. When my brother Harry was diagnosed with leukemia over a decade ago, he survived because of our sister. She was the donor for his bone marrow transplant at Memorial Sloan Kettering Cancer Center in New York. That's the meaning of family, unconditional mutual trust and respect, and being there when you're needed most.

My fervent hope for my children when they become parents is to nurture spiritually, emotionally, and intellectually healthy children. Sherry and I are now grandparents to two beautiful daughters of Sam and Linda. They are expecting another one this year. We look forward to becoming grandparents to more children someday and transmitting the values we hold dear to a new generation.

Chapter 14

HAPPINESS, LEADERSHIP, AND A PHILOSOPHY OF LIFE

There are no such beings as consistently happy people. Instead, there are *happier* people. Given the satisfaction and joy I've experienced and described about my life, including my career, family, and travels, that may seem like an odd statement, but being happy all the time is an unrealistic goal. I'm grateful to be *happier*; it's a positive state of mind that I choose and cherish.

Pain, frustration, anger, suffering, humiliation, disappointment, and other unpleasant feelings and setbacks are part of the human experience. Being happier means knowing how to deal with those feelings. It's impossible to feel truly happy if you've never felt pain or never been unhappy. Whether it's a career or relationship failure, happier people are those who are resilient, bounce back, and learn from life's challenges. Instead of giving up, they move forward and try again.

I've described my successes at length but have only touched briefly upon my failures, and there are many. My failures became catalysts for me to change and improve. For example, the high schools I attended, Delhi Public School and Yadavindra Public School, were both heavily sports-oriented, and I was not very athletic. I felt dejected when I couldn't score at cricket games as my friends did, but my lack of athleticism as a youth motivated me to find a sport I enjoyed and did well. Now, my passion is golf, and I'm determined to play the top 100 courses in America and the world. It's a great game for socializing and business networking and promotes the interpersonal skills of respect, encouragement, and courtesy.

Additionally, my academic limitations motivated me to discover and make the most of how I learn best. As a youth, I was a B+ student, which was particularly disappointing because my older brother got all A's. However, my parents reassured me that I might be poor at memorization, but I had another critical learning skill: I was intellectually curious and tried to delve into the meaning behind information, not just parrot back facts. I've been a lifelong learner, attending schools and institutions of higher learning, YPO forums, and universities, reading voraciously, writing, and listening to podcasts and lectures.

On a personal level, it hurts me even now to think how I upset Sherry just after we got married. A young bride going to live in a foreign country, she very much wanted to go on a honeymoon, but I chose to visit my cousin instead. My problem was a lack of empathy; instead of looking at Sherry's point of view, I favored my feelings. Now, I strive to actively listen to and respect others' perspectives, whether or not I agree with them.

I wasn't immune to business failures either. My first performance review at American National Bank was extremely upsetting. I had left First Valley Bank to accept the position at American National, and the CEO, Jeff Lord, told me my Indian accent was a significant problem. I was taken aback but determined to improve. What did I do? I found a speech therapist in downtown Manhattan and drove there from Morristown, New Jersey, three days a week for four months for therapy sessions. Even though the therapist said I should be proud of my accent, I was on a mission of self-improvement, which was spurred by an openness to feedback.

My biggest financial setback was after building Sovereign Bank. I mismanaged my personal affairs and lost practically all my hard-earned money. But I was resilient and moved on to another opportunity, building Customers Bank and enjoying the financial rewards. My position also gives me a very special opportunity to work with my son, Sam.

Through failure and disappointment, we learn to manage our expectations, and, in so doing, we become happier. Happiness is a state of mind. I think of the little kids in the middle of the desert in Afghanistan playing happily on the dirt road as if they didn't have a care in the world. They were excited simply to see strangers pass through. Those kids weren't focused on what they lacked; they found happiness in what they had.

Similarly, one time, Sherry and I were chatting with the driver in a taxi in Hawaii. He was overjoyed by what many would consider a minor occurrence; he had made an extra $5 on his first fare that morning. To him, it was a windfall and a great start to his day.

To appreciate success, you need to encounter failure first-hand. To appreciate happiness, you need to experience unhappiness. Again, it's a matter of managing your expectations. A critical element of being happier is feeling and expressing gratitude, which is precisely what the taxi driver did.

My thoughts on happiness are influenced by Tal Ben-Shahar's teachings, along with my own experiences.[2] Ben-Shahar is an Israeli-born lecturer and writer who earned a bachelor's degree in psychology and philosophy and a Ph.D. in organizational behavior at Harvard University. He also created and teaches a course there that made history. His class, "Positive Psychology," is the largest, most popular one ever at Harvard. One in five students take his course! Luvleen attended his class as a Harvard student and introduced Sherry and me to him.

Ben-Shahar defines happiness as "the overall feeling of both pleasure and meaning in your life."[3] It's when you feel pleasure in the here and now *and* do something that you'll find meaningful in the long run. Ben-Shahar designed a matrix, "the hamburger model," to illustrate his ideas. A perfect hamburger is one that is delicious (present benefit) *and* healthy (future benefit).

He applies this concept to both relationships and workplaces. A healthy relationship is one where you enjoy being together now *and* are building a future. In the workplace, it's enjoying your daily work *and* experiencing a sustainable sense of purpose and meaning.

I endorse Ben-Shahar's ideas and know I've repeated my conviction that it's critical to find purpose and meaning in life by continually developing emotionally, intellectually, and spiritually. I repeat it in this book and in my speeches. I repeat it to my employees, friends, and children. Why? Because this philosophy permeates who I am and how I live my life. It's been my constant signpost on the road to happiness and fulfillment.

Meditation is one way to nurture gratitude and spirituality. I had the

---

[2] https://www.youtube.com/watch?v=wBWejfL0xOA

[3] https://www.youtube.com/watch?v=IJ5Qr5Rdaf4

privilege of learning meditation at Banaras University from Maharishi Mahesh Yogi. He created the silent mantra technique transcendental meditation and became the Beatles' and other celebrities' idol. When I meditate, I can feel the stress leaving my body.

I also achieve a sense of spiritual well-being through physical exercise. My wife and I try our best to walk a mile or two daily, and we feel its benefits. Notice I say, "try." We don't always achieve our goal, but as with any goal, you must try and do your best to work at it.

❁❁❁

I want to revisit the topic of leadership. Not only because it is vital to me but also because Ben-Shahar's principles of happiness also apply to maximizing satisfaction and productivity in the workplace. Of course, my observations are empirical, not scientific, but many align with Ben-Shahar's principles.[4]

To be a great leader, you must first be a great human being. Listening to diverse views and accepting feedback are hallmarks of mature people, which is a prerequisite for effective leaders. To do so, it's necessary to develop self-awareness to understand your behavior and its impact on others. Self-awareness is also a requirement for understanding others' behavior and perspectives. According to Ben-Shahar, the number one quality of extraordinary leadership is active listening. Extraordinary leaders are fully present and empathetically responsive.

Leadership is often confused with management. Many graduate schools of business, even prestigious universities, have the word "management" in their names. It was a conscious decision to name the Wilkes business school "The Sidhu School of Business and *Leadership*." Leadership is a highly interpersonal endeavor; after all, leaders lead people. Some mistakenly believe that leadership skills are something that you're born with. No! They can be taught, developed, and continually improved.

Wilkes' holistic approach to leadership, combining personal and professional

---

[4] See Talbenshahar.com and Potentialife.com

development, is mirrored in the YPO forums that I've attended for thirty years. YPO forums bring together small groups of executives forming a "personal board of directors" who discuss their actual experiences on four topics, namely self, family, business, and spirituality. The moderator rotates from year to year. Each participant is given a few minutes to describe their previous thirty days and their expectations for the next thirty days or so. It's a marvelous exercise in trust (everyone has signed a confidentiality agreement), respectful listening (no one can interrupt a presentation), asking clarifying questions, and giving constructive feedback. At Sovereign Bank, we held team forums modeled on YPO concepts.

My YPO forum colleagues are more like my "brothers." We have mutually respectful, authentic relationships with each other. In addition to attending my monthly local Pennsylvania forums, I've had the privilege of participating in an international group that meets regularly in different cities in Europe and the US. Who could have predicted that my meeting as a youth with India's Prime Minister Indira Gandhi would presage a lifetime of meetings with leaders worldwide?

The international YPO meetings are phenomenal learning experiences, and it is inspirational to meet world leaders. We once met a Sant'Angelo in Vatican City, where I asked for forgiveness for bringing an open bottle of wine into St. Patrick's Cathedral. Other highlights include having dinner at Princess di Gangi's palace in Palermo, meeting a Russian minister at the Kremlin, the prime minister of Ukraine in Kyiv, Prime Minister Iatina in Pisa, the deputy prime minister and several members of parliament in London, the head of the World Bank in Paris, the president of Switzerland at his "hut" in the Alps, Yassar Arafat in Palestine, Israeli Prime Minister Shimon Peres, and His Holiness the Dalai Lama in Dharamsala, India.

In Salzburg, we took part in a simulated pilot training, visited "Eagles Nest," and stayed at Smith Haut Lafitte Vineyards in Bordeaux, where we were told, "you can make millions with wine, but you have to start with billions." Additionally, we experienced the only rainy day in the Sahara desert in southern Morocco and flew out of a military base in the middle of the night to Paris. Most important were the deep friendships I developed with folks from all over the world.

Of course, in Pennsylvania, my friendships with my YPO "brothers" are even more intimate since we see each other regularly, spending three to four days together annually at a retreat. I feel privileged and grateful to have met such wonderful human beings through local, national, and international YPO forums.

As I've said, leadership can be learned. And as they say, you don't just talk the talk; you walk the walk. A leader must model the value of continuing education. The Harvard Executive Education CEO program and Young Presidents' Organization' forums get it right, and they complement each other.

I discussed these programs earlier, but I want to expand on why they are so impactful. Harvard's case study approach to business education focuses on real-life examples and integrates practical applications of theory. What better way to learn about business and leadership than to be immersed in actual scenarios and exchange ideas with a diverse group of peers? YPO also provides opportunities to engage with a variety of peers, share ideas and experiences, and develop authentic friendships. The result is openness to listening to varied perspectives and developing the interpersonal skills and respectful relationships that are the hallmarks of effective leaders.

In my opinion, Harvard and other top-tier schools and YPO forums develop great leaders. How? They nurture the four essential traits that I'm passionate about. (1) they have clarity about their mission or purpose, (2) they possess internal mastery, (3) they are masters of their external environments, and (4) they have a passion for continuous improvement.

Let me elaborate further on what these four invaluable qualities mean. I've never ever given up on strengthening them myself and will continue to do so.

Clarity about mission or purpose. My father's mindset as a military leader taught me the importance of defining your vision and the strategic steps required to achieve it. That's the responsibility of a leader. A great leader is skilled at setting the direction and operational foundation for the organization. Some thinkers and educators use different terminology to express this concept, for example, "goal" refers to the long-term mission, and "objective" refers to the measurable steps to reach it.

The key is to set milestones to reach along the way and continually evaluate your progress. Furthermore, everyone on your team must be clear on the mission so that all members are equipped to give the same answer to the question, "What is our mission?" Team members also need to understand their role in fulfilling it. This knowledge creates alignment.

Internal mastery. Leaders must be experts in internal mastery, meaning being aware of what is happening in areas they can control, including themselves. What are we good at and not good at? What are our strengths and weaknesses? How are we using our systems? Are we selecting the right people and assigning them to the right roles? Are we effectively encouraging and building people? Most importantly, are we focusing on the three or four things that will get us the best results?

All these questions require awareness and reflection. They promote engagement. Sometimes, it's necessary to pivot and change course, so a leader must encourage agility to achieve the best outcomes.

External mastery. Just as leaders need to be aware of the internal environment, they need to understand the external environment. Factors outside their control affect them tremendously. This holds true for sports, companies, and even relationships. Change is a constant, and adaptation is a key requirement.

A great leader can adapt to factors outside their control. How is the economy? What are state-of-the-art technological advances? How are customers' expectations changing? How is the media influencing trends? Most significantly, what are the opportunities, and what are the threats? Awareness of the external environment, like awareness of your internal environment, must also translate into pivoting when necessary.

Passion for continuous improvement. Throughout this book, I've advocated for lifelong learning in the emotional, intellectual, and spiritual domains. It's an essential trait for becoming a mature human being. Happier people and superlative leaders exhibit this passion for learning.

Great leaders apply these four principles within their organizations. For example, we get our teams together at Customers Bank to engage in exercises that strengthen personal and professional development. We discuss and clarify our mission and engage in self-assessments. Everyone has an opportunity to express their opinions in a non-judgmental atmosphere. These meetings aim to promote team members' mastery of the internal environment.

Similarly, there are ways to develop mastery of the external environment. At Sovereign Bank, we would ask the tellers, not the branch managers, to go out and shop at our competitors and report back to us. What was happening at other banks' branches? What could we do better? The tellers' visits engaged them in actively learning about our external environment. The task also empowered them and provided an opportunity for their professional development.

Another essential quality of a superlative leader is the ability to take complex ideas and make them simple. Much like a military mission commander must focus on what matters most, business leaders must focus on what's critical. A business will thrive if the leader articulates a clear, measurable vision and mission, along with a strategy to achieve it, and defines four or five critical success factors that will make 90 percent of the difference. In contrast, setting dozens of goals often makes a company rudderless and yields mediocrity.

In my opinion, a bank CEO should specifically focus on the four critical success factors I outlined earlier. These are the principles we applied to transform the failing Penn Savings Bank into the hugely successful Sovereign Bancorp. They are pretty much the same or similar to the standards we currently apply at Customers Bank: (1) high asset quality, (2) low-interest rate risk coupled with a strong risk management culture, (3) high levels of productivity and low-efficiency ratios, and (4) continually improving service excellence with an emphasis on team members. Implementing this formula for success requires you to take a step further and apply assessment.

How do you assess whether you're doing a good job at achieving your critical success factors? The book *In Search of Excellence* by Tom Peters and Robert Waterman, which I read some thirty years ago, draws from research by McKinsey. It examines how some companies succeed while others fail in the same industry.

Peters and Waterman developed 7-S, a set of ideals that successful company leaders should focus on.[5] These standards provide a framework for what is necessary to achieve your goals. They need to be aligned throughout the organization and continually evaluated.

The framework's foundation is straightforward: keep complex things simple. Much like people need to engage in self-assessment to develop and improve, business leaders need to engage in organizational assessment to grow. Again, it's essential to be reflective and open to evaluation and feedback.

The 7-Ss of Peter's and Waterman's model are: (1) strategy, (2) staff, (3) skillset, (4) systems, (5) style, (6) structure, and (7) shared values. I've added an eighth component that you're familiar with by now: self-awareness. (I would have preferred to call this "emotional maturity," but an "E" seemed out-of-place.) The 7-Ss are intended to focus the leadership on what's important.

Let's examine each parameter more closely. Assessment requires continually asking the right questions before, during, and after. But that's not enough. Once you've determined the answers, it's imperative to reflect and correct.

Strategy. Is there absolute clarity about your strategy? Are there appropriate benchmarks in place to evaluate whether the company is moving in the right direction?

Staff. Do you have the right people in the right roles? How are teams functioning? Are your employees furthering or stymying your mission? Are they engaged?

Skillset. Do your staff members possess the right skill sets? Are there gaps in their competencies? These questions do not refer to the company's various job descriptions. That's the function of management. A leader ensures that jobs are getting done by people who have the skills to get them done.

Systems. Are your systems relevant to your mission? Will they help to execute it? This broad parameter ranges from manufacturing systems to

---

[5] https://www.mindtools.com/pages/article/newSTR_91.htm

communication systems to compensation systems. Each dimension needs to be appropriate, efficient, and effective.

Style. How does your company manage its people? How do you communicate with them? Are you encouraging a culture that not only facilitates your goals but is also consistent with the four standards strategy, staff, structure, and style?

Structure. What is the company's hierarchy? Will the organizational structure facilitate the achievement of your mission? Who reports to whom? How do employees interact? Are your teams cohering?

Shared values. What is the company's culture? What are its priorities? Are the values strong across all strata of the organization? Is there mutual trust and respect?

Careful, continual assessment, in other words, self-awareness, of these standards is the purview of an organization's leadership; however, the EQ mindset needs to be transmitted and developed throughout to create a culture of achievement. That's what I did at Sovereign, and that's what I'm doing at Customers.

Roman Emperor Marcus Aurelius was quoted as saying, "perfection of character is this: to live each day as if it were your last." Guru Granth Sahib, Sikh's most spiritual book, says the same. As I've gotten older, I have a better understanding of what this means. The attitude of carpe diem infuses my emotional, intellectual, and spiritual life. It's all about balance and focus. It makes me happier.

❋❋❋

As I enter the last chapter of my life, I'm excited about my vision for the next few years, may God grant me to live.

- I want to give back to the youth I touch as much as possible. Of course, I'll start with my family, but my real value would be to help make my children and grandchildren intellectually, emotionally, and spiritually better than me. That way, they will hopefully become authentic leaders and will keep giving back to help those in need.

- I want to see more of the world and travel with my wife Sherry and other family members. Hopefully, I'll immerse myself more in different cultures and learn from diverse people. I want to continue on the *tonga* ride that began just before I was born!
- I wish to remain active and passionate about the sport of golf. I dream of playing at most of the top 100 golf courses in America and the world.
- I want to do everything possible to make my business ventures built to last, contribute to the local communities they serve, and provide value to our customers and investors/ shareholders.

God willing, I will make my vision a reality.

❁❁❁

Victor Frankl's book *Man's Search for Meaning* has significantly impacted my life over the years. I read it for the first time as a student at Wilkes University and believe it is one of the century's greatest books, and it has stood the test of time.

Besides describing his experience in a Nazi concentration camp, Frankl focuses on the importance of human beings' need to have a meaning to keep living. The search for meaning can lead to different outcomes for different people, but finding meaning is essential to life. Frankl also discusses how people may have little control over what happens, but they have the freedom to choose how they will respond and deal with a situation.

In many ways, my father's views were similar to Frankl's. He believed that being clear about what you want to do, your vision and mission, and strategies to achieve them, is of paramount importance. He also felt it is essential to understand yourself and the circumstances you are dealing with. To always look forward to something significant to do. To be passionate about continuous improvement. To be wholeheartedly committed to realizing your vision. And to never ever ever give up.

Family Reflection

SAM SIDHU

As Jay Sidhu's son, I'm thankful that he has shared his story with you on these pages. I've had the privilege of growing up learning about his life and being inspired by him as my ultimate role model. His influence on my life is profound and far-reaching. People ask me what it's like to work alongside him at Customers Bank. The answer is simple. It's a pleasure and an honor.

My father exposed me to the business world when I was just ten or eleven. He would bring me with him to the office on weekends while he caught up on work or signed documents. One time, I told him he had an easy job since all he did was sign his name. He set me straight. My comment led to a conversation that gave me a broader understanding of what it means to operate in the business world and certify regulatory filings.

Thanks to my father, I learned first-hand about the inner workings of a bank, meeting board members and sometimes even sitting in on meetings. My father also introduced me to the social and networking aspects of business (and golf). I attended offsite management meetings and investment banker dinners. These experiences promoted my ability to absorb information and understand interpersonal interactions. Of course, at times, I was bored, but I gained sophisticated communication skills beyond my age. I also gained insight and admiration for how my father comported himself in various business settings.

My father did more than expose me to his work life; he also encouraged me in directions I would otherwise not have pursued. He didn't push; instead, he pointed. For example, when I was in high school, he suggested I set up a business. I set up a limited liability company, an education in itself, and launched Brandhaven.com, selling overrun clothing on the gray market. We made tens of thousands of dollars in revenue, which sounds betters than it was. The number wasn't *annual* revenue, it was *total* revenue, and we had tens of thousands of dollars in expenses. But my foray into entrepreneurship was invaluable.

As you've read, my father places a high value on education. He set the bar high, and I shared his drive to excel. My top-notch formal education at the Wharton School at The University of Pennsylvania and Harvard Business School supplemented my father's informal lessons.

I developed an interest in private equity investment and, in keeping with my entrepreneurial spirit, established Megalith Financial Acquisition Corp. after graduating from Harvard. I sat on the board of Customers Bank and, as my father has described, joined Customers Bank as President and CEO in early 2020.

My father's lessons on leadership also strongly impacted me. I emulated his style of fostering decentralized autonomy in an organization, allowing team members to figure things out instead of micromanaging them. He taught me why and how one role of C-suite executives was eliminating bureaucracy whenever and wherever possible. He also taught me through his example about agility and perseverance. He doesn't just *say*, "never ever give up," he *demonstrates* it.

On a more personal level, I admire the guts and smarts it took my father to hitchhike across Asia and Europe as a kid. One time, as our family flew over a route in Italy he had traversed, he pointed out how today, what he did would be impossible. Further, he hitchhiked with no money and came to America with no money. He exemplifies the American Dream and the meaning of a self-made man.

Although I had a modest upper-middle-class upbringing, my father worried that my exposure to the high-flying corporate world of private planes, fine dining, luxury accommodations, and fancy golf outings would give me a distorted sense of entitlement. He did everything possible to demonstrate the value of honest hard work and humility. For example, when our family traveled to India, my sister Luvleen and I would sit in economy while my parents sat in business class. He made sure we didn't have a sense of unearned privilege.

I owe my father a debt of gratitude. His example and his lessons have transformed my life.

Sam Sidhu
President and CEO of Customers Bank
President of Customers Bancorp

Family Reflection

LUVLEEN SIDHU

My dad is one of the biggest blessings of my life. He has a zest for life, a passion for business, a spirit of optimism, and a commitment to spiritual and authentic living. I am forever grateful for his positive influence. My dad instilled in me an appreciation for how enriching life can be. How your attitude and thinking determine eighty percent of what you do, and only twenty percent is luck or strategy. The attitudes and actions my dad describes in this book are 100 percent consistent with the man I know.

He taught me the importance of always having a vision and goals in mind and never giving up on achieving them, despite obstacles. He frequently reminded me that tough times don't last, but tough people do. My dad has taught me that gratitude lightens your burdens so you can think more clearly and live more fully.

As with my brother, my dad encouraged me to follow my dreams and stretch beyond my potential. When I needed more challenging classes in middle school, he suggested I take courses at the high school. When I considered pursuing medicine, he suggested I form a club at school or set up a women's healthcare camp in India, which I did as an 11th grader. When I wanted to attend Harvard, he suggested I do everything humanly possible to make that happen.

My dad nurtured my interest in banking and my entrepreneurial goals. It was a natural progression in our relationship for us to work together professionally. When I'm asked how this collaboration can possibly work, there's one answer: mutual trust and respect. It's a tribute to my father that both my brother and I have worked closely with him in business.

When I graduated from Harvard University, my dad and I continued our ongoing discussion of the future of banking in light of the changing landscape of technology. We came up with the idea of BankMobile, a banking model that leveraged technology and didn't rely on branches. We believed this concept would appeal to students and recognized that people were often loyal to their first bank. Here was a way to gain lifelong customers.

Eight years later, BankMobile became BM Technologies, Inc., a publicly traded NYSE financial technology (fintech) company. I was the youngest female cofounder and CEO to take a company public. I credit my dad for his constant guidance in accelerating the path of my career trajectory. I'm blessed to have him as my mentor, and I believe I have a bright future, both personally and professionally. As dad says, you always have something significant left to do.

My dad instilled in me a strong sense of spirituality. Our family went to a Sikh temple where he taught history every Sunday. Dad showed me that Sikhism is a way of life, a set of values to live by. He taught me to choose to live my life in a truthful, authentic way. To give 100 percent in whatever realm of life I choose, to give it my all, and then let go and surrender.

My dad exemplifies his credo of making the impossible possible. I admire how he bravely hitchhiked through Asia and Europe to spread a message of peace through mutual understanding. When I was young, we'd look at maps together, and he'd trace his route with a finger and humbly describe how the spiritual guru Guru Nanak also journeyed to preach a message of equality.

As my dad would say, he still has something significant yet to do. And so do I.

Luvleen Sidhu
Chair, CEO & Founder of BM Technologies, Inc.

Appendix

CUSTOMERS BANK HOLIDAY GREETING

Happy Holidays!
Dear Fellow Team Members:

It was great to see many of you at our holiday parties after months of isolation. I love this time of the year. From Thanksgiving to Hanukah and through Christmas into New Year's Day, we have opportunities for getting together with family and friends to celebrate the year and offer our gratitude. It's amazing how time flies and that 2022 is already right around the corner.

As we reflect on 2021, Sam and I want to express our deep appreciation and gratitude for all your hard work and commitment during a difficult period. You made 2021 a year of extraordinary accomplishments. We believe we are also set up for what we hope to be an excellent year ahead.

During 2021, we celebrated many successes and learned from some of our challenges. No teams or companies want to fail, but only a select few do exceptionally well consistently. It's the people who create winning teams through teamwork, setting aggressive goals, working hard, working smart, having fun, and focusing on and following through on priorities. Consistently exceptional teams have a will to succeed and an unwavering commitment to the principles of integrity, mutual trust, and respect. When a consistently exceptional team faces adversity or challenges, they figure out the issues and get back to moving forward. They never ever give up.

These are the qualities of consistent winners. These are the qualities of Customers Bank. We feel so privileged to be a part of this winning team. Thank you for all you do each day for our customers, our fellow team members, the communities we serve, and as a result, our shareholders.

Much of our recent success can be attributed to our response to the global pandemic and our responsibility to quickly deliver PPP loans to businesses in need. We partnered with fintechs, crafting a hybrid model that brought the best of tech firms and experienced commercial bankers to bear on the problem. Ultimately, we surpassed the productions of Bank of America, Citi Group, Chase, and all the "big banks." I am so proud that we were the second highest ranking PPP lender by number of loans with over 320,000 loans, worth about $10.0 billion, and saved an estimated one million jobs! Through our "white label" product, Customers Bank was among the nation's top lenders to minority-, woman-, and veteran-owned businesses. We will make many of these firms "customers for life."

With your help, we met or exceeded practically all our goals despite a challenging environment. Here are some examples of our teams' many accomplishments:

a. Our "Business and Private Banking" teams in PA/NJ, Metro New York, New England, and other areas increased outstanding commercial loans (excluding PPP) from about $3.5 billion a year ago to about $4.1 billion at the end of 2021, a growth of over 17% in one year. Deposits from these teams and other efforts grew from $7.1 billion a year ago to about $10.3 billion at the end of 2021, an exceptional achievement. Our national businesses, including the commercial finance team based in New Hampshire, the specialty finance team that works principally out of New York, the fund finance team, the healthcare teams, and the newly acquired technology and venture capital team are executing their strategies brilliantly. We have also set some aggressive goals for the National SBA Lending division.
b. Our "Banking the Mortgage Company," another nationwide business for the bank, held outstanding commercial loans at about the $2-3 billion range throughout the year. In addition, the demand deposits and fee income from these clients continued to make this team one of the most profitable in the bank.
c. Our "National Consumer Lending" team built our business from $1.3 billion to $1.7 billion and added new initiatives to increase fee income.

d. We adjusted the strategies for our "Multi-Family and CRE" teams. They are working hard on developing new opportunities for multi-family and structured CRE loans. Kudos to the teams for meeting or exceeding our revised goals for them.
e. Our credit, risk management, compliance, fair & responsible banking, audit, finance and treasury, operations and technology, special assets, security, team member services, CRA, mortgage banking, servicing, and other support teams all worked hard and collaborated to maintain our strong risk management and credit profile. Their attention to detail and service makes us a better bank and makes our customers say, "WOW!"
f. In mid-October, we announced the soft launch of a new real-time, blockchain-based instant payment system for our business customers. We are only the third bank in America to offer such a service. We believe that, in the long-term, providing an instant payment platform will be "table stakes" for serious commercial banks. We foresee interest from manufacturing and retail supply chains, logistics and transportation, construction, and even large-scale business services like IT and engineering. However, in the immediate period, interest came from the crypto industry. Our initial clients began the onboarding process, BSA, AML, and KYC, in September, bringing $1.5 billion to the bank in mostly no-cost deposits. Our inaugural institutional crypto clients are among the premier cryptocurrency and digital asset institutions, making the bank one of the nation's leading financial services providers in the growing global crypto industry.
g. "Team Member Services" worked with others in the company, and especially the COVID-19 task force, to meet the challenges of the pandemic and work from home. The Code of Commitment codified our responsibilities to and respect for one another. Despite the challenges, TMS and our learning coaches are onboarding new talent, engaging team members through the Office Vibe tool, advancing our culture, and, with the invaluable assistance of the EDIFY Council,

keeping us focused on the imperatives of diversity and inclusion. Congratulations to TMS for winning the "Healthiest Employer" award from the *Philadelphia Business Journal.*

h. We capped the year with the roll-out of our new brand identity. We gave ourselves a makeover with a fresh, crisp look in keeping with the tech-forward financial services company we have become. This was a big effort that will continue in the months ahead and which epitomizes our very bright future.

We are excited about 2022 and beyond. Back in 2019, we had set a goal to achieve about $6 in earnings per share by 2025 with a commensurate stock price in the $60s. We are on track to achieve a $6 EPS much sooner, and, as you know, our stock price rose over 250% in the past twelve months making CUBI one of the best-performing stocks in the US. Some analysts now have a CUBI price target of $100/share by the end of next year.

We are very pleased to make every one of you a shareholder in 2021. At the holiday parties, we announced that every team member would receive ten shares of CUBI. Hopefully, you will build upon this by participating in the Employee Stock Purchase Plan, which gives you an opportunity to buy Customers Bancorp stock at a 15% discount. We have never been more optimistic about our future for Customers Bank and Customers Bancorp, Inc., and we look forward to working with you to achieve our goals over the coming years.

All of us, including the board of directors, are very grateful and thankful to all our fellow team members for all you do each and every day so we all can succeed. Let's reach out to all our customers and shareholders and thank them for all their support.

Let's remember in our prayers all those who are suffering and in need. We are so proud of all of you who connect with those in need through United Way and other charities as donors and as volunteers helping to feed the elderly, supply blood for the sick and injured, shelter the homeless, educate our children, and support our veterans. Let's also remember our fellow countrymen and women who are still serving in many dangerous parts of the world so we can have a safer tomorrow.

Please call or email Sam or me anytime with questions or suggestions on how we can become a better bank. We hope to see many of you in the office regularly as we resume normalcy.

Wishing you and your family a Merry Christmas, Blessed Kwanza, and Happy New Year!

May all of you and your families have peace and prosperity throughout the new year, happiness that multiplies, health that we can be grateful for, fun around every corner, energy to chase our dreams, and joy to fill our holidays and the coming year.

With gratitude,
Jay Sidhu

Appendix

COMMENCEMENT REMARKS, PENN STATE UNIVERSITY

Penn State University – Berks Campus

Saturday, May 4, 2019

Jay Sidhu - Commencement Remarks

It is with great pleasure that I join you today on this historic occasion in your lives. First of all, please join me in saluting and congratulating your parents and others who have supported you, encouraged you, prayed for you, and worked hard for some of you to pay your tuition and expenses. Please give them a round of applause.

Also, the friendships you have developed here and the relationships you have built can be very meaningful throughout your life. Please congratulate the person on your left and right. Better yet, give them a hug and say, "congratulations, and God bless you."

Like you, I feel fortunate and privileged to have gone to a small school in Pennsylvania, Wilkes University, located just about eighty miles from here. I can never forget that part of my life, and I am still very much affiliated with Wilkes.

I asked my daughter what I should say today. She said, "Dad, don't try to be intelligent, funny, or charming. Just be yourself!" So in a simple, straightforward way, in less than 10 minutes, are my beliefs about the top four things that matter the most for a successful professional life. These are simply based on my life experiences at Wilkes and beyond, and I hope many of you might find them of interest.

First, to be successful in life, you must have a vision or a dream and a plan to achieve that vision.

I believe that the future is not something we just enter. The future is something we create with God's help. You must visualize and dream this future. If you don't know what you want, mediocrity is what you will get.

When I graduated from high school in India, I dreamed about traveling through most of Asia and Europe to promote world peace through understanding people. I had no money. But in pursuit of that dream, opportunities arose, and my roommate and I were successful in hitchhiking through today's hot spots like Afghanistan, Iran, and Iraq and then on to Turkey, Greece, Italy, Switzerland, France, England, Belgium, Holland, Germany, Austria, Yugoslavia, Albania, and back to India through Turkey, Iran, and Afghanistan. We found a way to do this over a three-month period on less than $100 total between the two of us and received the best education of our lives.

Then I had a vision of coming to the United States to study. I did not have money to even pay for the application fees. I applied to forty-two universities, pleading with them to look at my application with no fee. Wilkes accepted me with a full scholarship. I now feel so grateful for that good fortune and feel privileged to give back to Wilkes and help take the Jay S. Sidhu School of Business and Leadership to the next level.

Then I set a vision to create a "bank of the future" headquartered here in Berks County, Pennsylvania. Fortunately, despite lots of odds against us and numerous failures along the way, we have been successful and have today built a bank that helped create about 30,000 jobs, provides digital banking to millions of college students across America and has partnered with T-Mobile to provide digital banking to Americans like it's never seen done before.

There were also numerous obstacles along the way. From time to time, things looked hopeless, and I'm sure you will experience that too. But persistence and drive to achieve your vision, fortunately, do prevail for those who never ever give up. Consider the story of this visionary man:

- He failed in business two times

- He was defeated in local and statewide elections twice
- He lost two young sons
- He was defeated for a seat in Congress and the Senate five times
- He was defeated for Vice President
- Finally, at age 51, he was elected as one of the nation's most prominent presidents --- Abraham Lincoln

So, I ask you to have a vision for your personal and professional life and pursue that vision with a passion. You are entering professional life during one of the most exciting periods – the Digital Revolution. It's full of opportunities, so go for it. Whatever is worth doing is worth doing well, and nothing ever is achieved without enthusiasm, persistence, and hard work.

My *second belief* is that true success in life comes from being emotionally and spiritually healthy and by being an authentic person.

I believe that you cannot be a great leader unless you are a great human being first, and you cannot be a great human being unless you are authentic. The same principles that apply to emotionally healthy families and emotionally healthy and authentic friendships and relationships also apply to teams and businesses. It does not matter whether you wish to pursue a career in business, government, not-for-profit, education, law, healthcare, or entrepreneurship. Your college education has only developed your IQ skills. Your successes in life will be mostly dependent upon your communication skills, listening skills, empathy, honesty, integrity, being genuine, constantly seeking feedback, having values --- or being authentic.

Socrates and Aristotle, centuries ago, spoke about the importance of self-awareness and knowing yourself. As they say, learn to know yourself, and you can stop living with a stranger. Imagine for a moment the person in your life you admire the most. Is it your parent, friend, faculty member, or coach? Ask yourself why. Is it because they are or were genuinely trusting, a great listener, always there when you needed them, selfless, humble, and yet confident? In other words, they were genuine; they had wisdom and maturity. Wisdom comes from being authentic, knowing yourself, being truthful, and, most importantly, listening to the life experiences of your parents, grandparents, mentors, and also your religious leaders.

So, I urge you to continue developing your emotional intelligence each day. Take the Dale Carnegie course or Tony Robbins course. There are so many ways you can achieve this.

The *third point* I want to make is to have a future full of opportunities tomorrow, exceed expectations in whatever you are doing today.

People often waste careers complaining about their teachers or bosses, or partners. Why not look inwardly and excel at adapting to the opportunity you have? Why not commit to doing the best job you can do today? Be the best student in high school, and you get the best opportunities in colleges; best in college opens more doors for careers. Similarly, in life, be the best you can be in whatever opportunity you have in your professional life, and you will get ahead. Also, be the best spouse or partner, and you will have a terrific family life. Only working hard, working smart, and having fun encourage a good future. So, always strive to be authentic and the best you can be today, and you will have a great opportunity tomorrow.

Lastly, become a constant lifelong learner and commit to helping others in need.

As Helen Keller said, "*You do not simply want to spend the rest of your life. You want to invest in it.*" The more one learns the more one realizes how little one knows. Let's be passionate about our hobbies and our professions. Let's read, watch, listen, see the world, and learn. Let's open our minds to limitless learning and expectations as long as we live. That will give us happiness, success, and peace. I ask the faculty and staff to do the same and not just look at teaching students what they do not know in different subjects. Philosopher John Ruskin said, "*Education is also about teaching people to behave as they should behave.*" In other words, let's help develop complete human beings to their fullest potential, not just graduate them with academic degrees.

We are among the most fortunate in the world to have been given citizenship in a country like no other on earth, providing possibilities like no place else on earth. But nothing is handed to you. You have the potential to earn it, depending upon your commitment and hard work. Use your education and your success in life, not just for yourself, but to help those still trapped in cycles of poverty and violence. Above all, never lose faith in America and its values of freedom and free enterprise. Its faults are yours to fix, not to curse.

So, Class of 2019, you have a great life ahead of you. Have a vision about your future, be authentic, be a constant learner, give back to others in need, work hard, work smart, have fun, learn from your failures and setbacks, and take full advantage of what this wonderful world has to offer.

Thank you, good luck, and God bless you all.

Left to right: My wife Sherry and I with our daughter Luvleen, her husband Brian, our son Samvir and his wife Linda

Jay Sidhu serves as Chief Executive Officer of Customers Bancorp, Inc., and Executive Chairman of Customers Bank. He has an extensive and recognized background in banking. Prior to joining Customers Bank, he served as the Chairman and Chief Executive Officer of Sovereign Bancorp, Inc. There, he grew the organization from an Initial Public Offering of $12 million to a market cap approaching $12 billion, crediting it as the 17th largest banking institution in the country.

Sidhu has received various recognitions in the industry, including Financial World's CEO of the Year, Turnaround Entrepreneur of the Year, and was named the Large Business Leader of the Year by the Chamber of Commerce. He has spoken at YPO Universities in Dubai and Hong Kong about Authentic Leadership and has also been a speaker at conferences around the world including Singapore, London, Sydney, Prague, Dubai, and all over the US.

Sidhu earned a Master of Business Administration from Wilkes University and graduated from the Harvard Business School's Leadership Course for CEO's.